SEVEN STORIES

EVERY SALESPERSON MUST TELL

GW00471337

MIKE ADAMS

KONA
PRESS

'*Mike Adams*' Seven Stories Every Salesperson Must Tell *is a brilliant handbook on storytelling for sales professionals that delivers the key elements missing in other works to make this highest form of selling both intuitive and actionable. Highly recommended!*'

James Muir. CEO Best Practice International
and author of *The Perfect Close*

'*Finally a book that calls out storytelling for its relevance, power and potential in the business world. Mike's honesty and expertise in nailing and teaching the finer points of the "perfect story" is a great guide for all levels of sales professional to hone and adapt their storytelling skills to gain relevance, credibility and significant business outcomes, as well as build better connections with customers and stakeholders... "when you listen to another's story carefully, with an open heart, the truth of the character shines through".*'

Cheryl Robertson. State Director – WA, Microsoft Australia

'*Mike Adams has written a timelessly brilliant book for everyone who seeks to lead, influence or sell. He makes the profoundly simple point that "You'll sell more and you'll sell better when you tell and share purposeful stories". Mike has real-world experience and has himself sold more than $1 billion of business. Selling is one of toughest professions and Mike explains exactly how "business storytelling is the master key that unlocks all stages of the buying and selling cycle". Masterful storytelling is how to get to the next level of influence and success. I highly recommend this book for anyone in leadership or sales, regardless of their level of experience.*'

Tony Hughes. CEO RSVP Selling and author of
The Joshua Principle and *Combo Prospecting*

'Of the thousands of sales books written every year only a few stand out as ground-breaking—only a few will stand the test of time. Mike Adams' book Seven Stories Every Salesperson Must Tell is one of those.

'As the title suggests it is peppered with compelling true stories that reinforce why storytelling is an essential sales skill and why we need to prepare and practise our seven stories. And most importantly, Mike tells us how. He provides a very clear and structured approach to creating, practising and delivering our stories, each at the appropriate time in the buying journey and sales process.

'This book is an outstanding read and the best sales storytelling book I have read.'

John Smibert. Founder Sales Masterminds APAC and CEO Custell Strategic Selling Group

'A highly practical and engaging guide to how storytelling can create both positive customer experience AND a competitive advantage in any crowded market. We all know storytelling works. Mike has provided the best guide to how to make it work I've seen in 30 years of sales globally.'

Dean Mannix. CEO SalesROI and SalesITV

'The ability of a salesperson to tell stories is extremely powerful. Mike Adams does an excellent job of providing a framework to lead sellers to success. He discusses the key elements of stories and the importance of sharing these with prospects, rather than boring case studies and bullet points. The bottom line: stories work! Adams shows how persuasive they can be when done right.'

Mike Shulz. President of RAIN Group and co-author of *Insight Selling*

Project management and text design by Michael Hanrahan Publishing
Cover design by Peter Reardon

All images used with permission. Image credits:

Front cover image: Crayon and pencil sketch by Megan Adams, from a photograph by Craig Moore from The English Fly Fishing Shop (www.flyfishing-flies.com)

Modified fly image page 9: Photo by Michael Svoboda, Getty Images, ID 164587281

Modified brain image page 20: Artist Alexandr Mitiuc, Dreamstime, ID 18894695

Modified fishing image page 59: Fly fishing trout fisherman, Getty Images, ID 458253697

Modified fish image page 113: Rapids Camp 136 by Abe Blair Photography

Modified fish image page 167: Trout in net: Image Barry Garner, Dreamstime, ID 45166961

Author photo: Peter Singer

Disclaimer

Contents

PART 3: FIGHT

PART 4: LAND

Foreword

by Mike Bosworth

Reading Mike Adams' *Seven Stories* has caused me once again to reflect on how I think about sales effectiveness.

My sales journey began in 1972, working for Xerox Computer Services (XCS) which was founded in 1969 by the great James S. Campbell. Most people know Xerox invented more technology that they never made money on than any other tech organisation. Desktop icons, the mouse, Ethernet, the list goes on. Most people don't know that Xerox Computer Services also invented cloud computing.

When I joined XCS in 1972 after serving in the military and graduating from Cal Poly, Pomona, we had 50 Los Angeles based customers communicating real-time transactions over dumb terminals in departments like cost accounting, fund accounting, payroll, production control and material control. In case you think Software as a Service is a new thing, our customers paid us for the usage of our applications, for storage on our disk drives, for reports by the print line and for transactions (every 'enter' was 2.2 cents).

If the customers didn't use our system, there was no revenue. Because of this revenue model, all XCS employees were focused on keeping those 50 customers online.

I went through the same six weeks of product demo school that our newly hired, experienced salespeople (mostly ex-IBM) went through. At the end of product school they went into sales. But I was hired to do the job nobody else wanted — help desk support. I was just 25.

It typically took those experienced former IBM salespeople between nine and fifteen months to make their first sale. My 20/20 hindsight tells me that it took them that long to figure out how the job titles we were calling on could use our product. Demo school did not teach product usage by job title.

Xerox was also ahead of its time in the way they on-boarded me. I was employee number 120, and within two months of joining, my wife and I were invited to dinner with senior managers and executives from sales, marketing, operations, finance and product development. During these dinners we shared stories about our individual paths to where we were now working. Through those interactions I formed an emotional connection with the heads of multiple departments. If I had an unhappy customer on the phone, I knew who to call.

After a year on the help desk, I got promoted to field application support specialist and got to 'convert' new manufacturing, distribution and city government customers onto our 'cloud' interactive accounting system. I helped them figure out the best ways to use our applications to do their jobs much better than they ever had before.

When I was 28, a sales manager asked me to try sales. I had two answers – *no!* And *hell no!* Reason one: I had a low opinion of many of our salespeople who sold their prospects features we didn't have in order to make sales — that I had to rescue. Reason two: my violent alcoholic father was a salesman who could not keep a job longer than six months.

A week later, that same manager, along with our manager, succeeded in persuading me to 'try' sales for six I agreed on the condition of keeping my application support salary, and I had it in writing that if I did not like sales I could have my old job back.

My biggest worry was 'I don't know how to sell', but I *did* know how dozens of job titles *used* our applications. And I knew how they had done their jobs before they had our system, how they did their jobs using our system, and the success metrics to prove the improvement. My real insecurity about selling was I didn't know how find prospects. I didn't know how to look for the people who should be looking for my product.

My sales manager knew he had to teach me how to prospect. That meant teaching me how to cold call. Back then, cold calling meant physically walking into the lobby of a manufacturing company and saying to the receptionist, 'My name is Mike Bosworth. I work for Xerox Computer Services and I'd like to speak to your materials manager.'

Eighty percent of the time, the materials manager would come out to the lobby to meet me (yes, 80 percent!). Number one reason? Curiosity. Xerox had a huge halo as a great, innovative company. They were curious about why someone from Xerox would want to talk to a materials manager and curious about new technology for manufacturing, pre internet.

When the materials managers came to the lobby to meet me, many would glance at their watch. I was 28, they were 48. I knew they were kicking themselves for coming out to the lobby to meet with a 'kid'.

Unlike other new sales hires though, I didn't ask if they'd like to see a demo. Instead, I would shake hands, confirm he was the materials manager, and ask, 'Can I share a short story about a materials manager who works less than a mile from here and who I've been working with for the past 18 months?' They all said 'yes' to the offer of a peer story (what's called a success story in *Seven Stories*).

I would then tell them the 90-second story of Ed Blackman.

Ed is the materials manager at Elpac Electronics. Elpac manufactures power supplies. I met Ed two years ago at an Orange County, California, industry meeting.

Ed had a very difficult job. He was experiencing massive shortages, which was impacting their production schedule. There were partially completed kits stacked all over his factory floor, and he had to deal with two bills of material for every power supply they made. Ed's boss, the VP Manufacturing, was not meeting the shipment schedule and their backlog was out of control. To top it off, their CFO was unhappy with the cost of carrying too much inventory. To say Ed was feeling pressured is an understatement.

It was obvious to Ed that he needed a better way to respond to major vendor delivery changes. When he discovered 18 months ago that our technology would let him pre-plan his production schedule *overnight*, he decided to take the risk of being the first Southern California company to implement our new materials requirements planning (MRP) system.

We are now 18 months into the MRP implementation with Ed. His inventory turns have gone from 1.9 to almost 5. His backlog has been eliminated. They are operating off *one* bill-of-material, and 95 percent of shipments to customers are on time. Ed is beyond pleased.

And then I would transition to: 'Enough about Ed. What's going on around here?'

The vast majority of times, the materials manager that I had known for less than three minutes would begin talking freely about his own struggles. (Back then, I never met a female materials manager.) Usually, I would get invited in to take a look at their operation.

Then I could begin tending their stories.

In my first five months on quota I sold more than anyone in the history of the company had sold in a full year. Management were scratching their heads. How can this kid, two years out of college, outsell every other salesperson?

When I was 29 years old, after just one year on quota, I was 'promoted' to sales manager. I had to move from LA to New Jersey and inherited four older salespeople. I went from hero to zero. Number one salesperson in the company to number last sales manager.

Luckily, when they put me on that plane to New Jersey, they told me they wanted me to fly back to HQ four to six times each year to do sales training and teach others the things I had been doing intuitively. I told them I didn't know how to do sales training so they sent me to learn our corporate sales methodology, PSS (Professional Selling Skills), inside and out. One thing that stuck from that program was, *you can't teach rapport*. Rapport is 'chemistry' and the chemistry between any two humans is unique.

Since then, through my Solution Selling and Customer Centric Selling days, the one area I *avoided* as a sales trainer was teaching sellers how to 'establish rapport'. I would spend literally thirty minutes out of a four-day workshop on the basics of not *blowing* your first impression—eye contact, avoiding stereotypical sales language, avoiding the trophies and props in the buyer's office, silence up front so the buyer can decide whether we get right down to business or have some 'small talk'. That was it. I stayed away from rapport because I had it in my head that it was not *teachable*. I taught people a system for managing their complex sales conversations and their complex sale cycles.

I founded Solution Selling in 1983 with the mission of helping my clients 'lift' the bottom 80 percent of their sales forces. Their top 20 percent sellers were doing fine, bringing in 80 percent of the sales revenue. Over the years, I know that the selling systems I created have dramatically improved the effectiveness of thousands of salespeople. My clients told me so. They also told me something twenty times over twenty years that my intellectual arrogance kept me from diagnosing and understanding: 'Mike, our top 20 percent salespeople *love* Solution Selling, but within two weeks of the workshop our bottom 80 percent quit using it.'

What they quit using were the discovery question templates that were the bedrock of both methodologies: intelligent questions written by the smartest people in their company so their salespeople could ask specific buyer-types about specific problems that our solutions can help them solve. Why on earth would a bottom 80 percent salesperson stop using them?

In 2008, Sales Benchmark Index published their latest findings on the '80/20 rule'. Of the 1,100 companies SBI indexed, the ratio was now 87/13. This hit me like a ton of bricks. Despite all my personal efforts, 25 years as a sales trainer and the efforts of the entire sales training industry, with all the CRM systems, sales processes, sales manager training, with all the marketing messaging, and with all the coaching, just *13 percent of salespeople brought in 87 percent of the revenue in 2008*. The best got better and the worst got worse.

Ouch!

If I had been as curious as I should have been, I would have noticed that the bottom 80 percent of sellers lacked the intuitive ability to connect and build trust, and that they were going to their discovery questions *prematurely*. They were great questions, but coming from a salesperson the client did not yet trust. Buyers were pushing back, sending the unspoken message: 'You don't know me well enough to ask me those questions!'

I would also have discovered that the top 13 percent were doing something *very* different from the rest, and that it had to be *intuitive* or we all would have found a way to institutionalise it.

I now know we can do a lot more than teach sellers to manage a complex sales process. We can *also* teach them how they can influence change more effectively by emotionally connecting with their buyers through *storytelling*. In 2012, with Ben Zoldan, I wrote a textbook on sales storytelling, *What Great Salespeople Do*.

Why story? Mike Adams will explain. I'll just say that for the past hundred and ninety thousand years, humans have used oral tradition to share tribal knowledge and influence people to do difficult things that need to be done. We've used story to lead, communicate, educate, warn, persuade, engage others, inspire and celebrate success. And to *connect emotionally*. Why are the leaders in virtually all professions good storytellers? Story is in our DNA.

Seven Stories is the book to help you put these ideas into the world, to show people how to learn and change. The power of story can help *all* sellers, not just the elite, to emotionally connect and build trust with their customers and buyers.

Mike Bosworth, Olga Washington
Best-selling author of *Solution Selling* and
What Great Salespeople Do

A note from the author

If there's a book that you want to read, but it hasn't been written yet, then you must write it.

Toni Morrison, American novelist

I'm not a keen fisherman. But last year, on a whim, I put twenty rainbow trout in our swimming pool for the winter. The plan was to feed them up and invite friends around to fish them out in October. The pool went green and then black, but I learned how to manage the water with bacteria. I loved the twice-daily feeding ritual, the trout hurling themselves out of the water and our dog Tikka going bananas watching them. Then disaster. An algae bloom killed them all and I spent two months and a warehouse of chemicals restoring the pool. On the flip side, I got the fishing metaphor idea for this book.

Let's face it, the world isn't waiting for a new book on sales and taking on a project like this really isn't me. I was the one looking for the easy path. In the hare and the tortoise race, I'd be the hare—and hares don't write books. But the hare got a bad rap, don't you think? Damned for eternity because of a minor tactical miscalculation. Who wants to be the plodding tortoise? Wouldn't you rather be the brilliant hare, with an alarm clock?

In these pages I mean to address an omission in sales instruction and inject some of the hare's pace into your selling efforts, to share the recipe for the sprinter's secret sauce so you can take every sales situation in your stride, hit your targets with ease, then kick back and take a nap. Of course, if you insist on also working hard, doing the fanatical grit thing, be my guest, you'll be unstoppable.

I'm a sceptic of books that start with 'the world is rapidly changing so you need to do this *new thing*'. Yes, the world is changing fast, so more than ever we need to appreciate what has always worked and will continue to work, regardless of technological change.

I'm interested in the question, what endures? Life, at home and at work, is certainly changing. We are bombarded by more distractions than ever before. Our electronic devices seem to demand our constant attention, so we find we no longer maintain eye contact in meetings, we crash into things when walking in the street and we sit distracted at stop signs long after the lights have turned green. Are we becoming dumb humans under the control of smart devices? One outcome is that it's increasingly difficult to gain and hold people's attention. But good stories hold our attention as they always have. We still love a good movie, we binge watch TV miniseries, novels are as popular as ever, and some happily construct entire story worlds through computer games and disappear in them for hours.

Stories have always been important in business, and today they are more important than ever because they capture the attention of our distracted customers. Learn to use sales stories effectively and you will be more persuasive. Much more persuasive. And that will have a big impact on both your business and your personal life. With good story skills you'll be in control, because your secret story chart will ensure you can navigate even the most difficult business journeys.

Here's a thought experiment. Imagine you have to sell for a new company in an industry that's completely foreign to you. If today you sell high technology, imagine selling cleaning services. If you sell legal services to government, imagine selling computer systems to Amazon. And you have no more than a layperson's understanding of your new industry.

I duly appoint you senior business development manager. You have a $20 million target and eight months in which to sell. What do you need to know to succeed? Before you complain that this assignment is unrealistic, impossible, you should know I've been there and done that four times in my selling career. I don't recommend it as a career path (unless you're a thrill-seeker), but it can be done. Every industry is a classroom, as all new salespeople discover. And as more industries are disrupted by technological change, increasing numbers of seasoned salespeople will find they need to tackle new industries to maintain their career.

What do you need to know about your new company, industry and customers to meet this challenge? What's essential, and how should you learn it? You may be thinking, *I'll need a crash course on all that technical stuff and the jargon.* That would take years, and you don't have time, but you'll be provided with technical experts. Think more fundamentally.

Everything you need is contained within the seven stories I'll introduce in this book. Learn these stories and you will succeed. By the way, it's unlikely your new company has prepared the stories, so you'll need to do a quick sprint to get them ready. No sweat! Eight months is plenty of time, and you'll still have room for that afternoon snooze …

Online training: We provide online training to help our readers and clients develop their own seven stories. Throughout the book I provide links to video training content. You'll need to provide an email address to access the indicated videos, otherwise they are free access. The full online training course is a paid course.

Introduction

After nourishment, shelter and companionship,
stories are the thing we need most in the world.

Philip Pullman, English novelist

When we join the business world, we set aside a communication method we learned and loved as children. This book is about reconnecting you with it. I want to reawaken in you something you always knew: that telling stories is the most powerful way to connect, communicate and learn in any context.

Stories are the secret weapon of the best salespeople. If you follow the steps in this book, you can join this select group, with the ability to tell the stories that will unlock possibilities for exciting new business. That's a wonderful thing, a piece of magic that very few can perform. People will look at you in wonder. How did you do that? Your career will open up. You'll create better business relationships and better outcomes for your clients. And you'll build a career on stories that you can look back on and delight in. That's been my experience writing this book. I have looked back on the events of my sales career, its successes and failures, and followed the thread of stories that shape a career and a life.

You are most likely to be reading this book if you are in sales and you want to understand how the best salespeople get the best deals, week after week, year after year. If you lead sales teams, this book is for you. If it's your responsibility to create new business, or you need to change your customer's mind or change your own organisation to generate new business, you'll find many answers here. The bigger the sale you need to make, the more valuable you will find this book, because the biggest deals lean hardest on the book's central premise, which is: *if you want to land a sale, become a master of the seven story types.*

But its value is broader in scope than that. Simply put, if you need to persuade, this book is for you, and we all need to sell sometimes, whether it's selling ourselves in a job interview or selling an innovation in our company. There's something here for everyone who wants to persuade another person to their point of view.

Hang on a second, you're thinking, *who is this guy anyway? Why should I listen to him?*

Have you heard the Indian fable of the six blind men who encounter an elephant for the first time and try to make sense of it?

It was six men of Indostan,
To learning much inclined,
Who went to see the elephant
(Though all of them were blind),
That each by observation
Might satisfy his mind.

John Godfrey Saxe's (1816–1887) version of
'The Blind Men and the Elephant'

'The elephant is a wall,' said one man who ran his hand over the elephant's side. 'No, it's a rope!' called out the one holding its tail. 'A tree trunk!' insisted the one holding the trunk. One by one, each shared his partial experience of the whole. So it is with selling. 'Selling is about relationships,' some say. 'No, it's about questions … closing techniques … social media … cold calling!' And on and on.

In my career as a global sales leader, I've touched every part of the elephant. I've personally closed more than US$1.3 billion worth of sales in the United Kingdom, Norway, Germany, Russia, Ukraine, Kazakhstan, Belarus, China, Japan, Vietnam, Malaysia, Indonesia, India, Australia, New Zealand, Canada and the United States. That included software, computer hardware, telecommunications equipment, hardware devices, professional services, facility services and industrial products. In most cases I knew nothing about those products and services when I first started selling them.

So I've been around the world, in many sales and marketing roles, and around many industries and companies. I'd guess I have sold in more sales situations than anyone you know. I know the pressure of having a quota to meet. But I've also been a technical sales specialist, marketing manager, head of technical sales, head of customer service, sales manager and head of sales across the oil and gas industry, mining, telecommunications, facility services, industrial products and business consulting sectors with blue-chip companies such as Schlumberger, Siemens, Nokia, Halliburton, Spotless and Motorola. I've chased monster deals that take years and transactional deals, many per month.

Among the successes (and failures) along the way, I'm most proud of the times my teams created something out of nothing, blowing away the sales target, making new friends and building real relationships in the process.

I don't want to give the impression that I'm a super-talented, natural-born sales god. The opposite is closer to the truth. I've had amazing good fortune and spent much of my career struggling to find a repeatable selling method.

The mobiliser

My first sales role was selling software to oil and gas companies more than twenty years ago in Norway. With six large oil companies as my assigned territory, I was working actively in three of them because I didn't see opportunity in the others. A colleague told me about a friend of hers who was working at one of my 'sleeper' clients and she suggested I meet him.

I found Martyn tucked away in a small office doing an extraordinary job. His company (one of the largest oil companies in the world) was a minor shareholder in a three-billion-barrel Norwegian oilfield, and Martyn's role was to check all the technical analyses and decisions made by the main operator. He was doing this on his own, by personally replicating the work of a team of dozens of diverse technical experts.

I showed Martyn our new software, which combined applications from many disciplines into one system. He thought it was fantastic and set about using it. But Martyn didn't just think it was good for himself, he thought his company should use our software—everywhere in the world. It happened that managers world-wide from Martyn's company were coming to Norway for a global conference. So I made our company auditorium available and Martyn prepared a software demonstration for the global group.

Martyn's father was a vaudeville actor, and he'd inherited a flair for showmanship. He performed a wonderful animated software demonstration, explaining what his problem was and showing what he had done with his oilfield. The impact was extraordinary. Martyn's company went on to purchase a global corporate licence—our first major corporate deal.

I remember sitting in the audience beside my boss, who'd flown over from England for the demonstration. At the end of Martyn's performance my boss turned to me with an astonished look on his face and said, 'Wow! That was amazing! Well done, Mike!' That moment launched my sales career.

It's hard to convey the extent of my good fortune. That chance meeting with Martyn, his being in exactly the situation that required our software, and the client's global meeting taking place, improbably, right where I was based. There are other factors. Martyn has a master of engineering from Cambridge University and a master of petroleum engineering. He's both bright and persuasive—and he's a maverick, willing to agitate for what he wants. He ended up joining our company, where he personally persuaded our CEO to make investments that built a new $1 billion per annum software business.

It's fair to say that I chanced upon a one in a million mobiliser![1] If you don't want to rely on that sort of luck, then read on.

By training, I'm an engineer. We engineers take an analytical approach to problem solving. We don't rest until we understand how something works. In detail! Once we've understood, we seek practical applications. For the twenty years I have been successful at selling, I've wanted to find the formula, and how to teach that to others. How come some people sell with ease, but most struggle? How to separate luck from good technique?

This was my quest. I studied with great sales training companies; Miller Heiman, InfoTeam, TAS, AchieveGlobal and Corporate Visions, and many smaller providers. They were great programs; each was valuable, but all of them looked at only part of the elephant. None provided the definitive answer because none included instruction on storytelling.

I read countless sales books — I have hundreds stacked in my office and dozens more on my Kindle. But the selling and buying theories they tout also fail to provide a complete answer. So I expanded my search, poring through books and papers on behavioural psychology, neuroscience and artificial intelligence (AI). It was a long journey, and the solution took me twenty years to uncover. But if you let me be your guide, you'll learn something new and transforming, and you won't need twenty years to find it. In a nutshell, my message is simple: You'll sell more and you'll sell better when you tell and share purposeful stories.

> **You'll sell more and you'll sell better when you tell and share purposeful stories.**

Finally, I felt ready to turn to training. Of course, I had trained hundreds of salespeople in my sales leadership roles, but since 2014 I have trained many more through the programs offered by our sales consulting company, Growth in Focus. We recorded sales conversations — hundreds of them — and analysed them, both manually and using AI speech analysis. I've watched and listened to those salespeople as they tried, and most often failed, to persuade. I've also observed the rare 'natural' storytellers weave their spell. Based on all of this painstaking research, and my own personal experience, I developed our 'Storytelling for Salespeople' program, which we have now taught to sales teams across Australia and internationally, and watched them grow and thrive. We've also facilitated public story workshops for hundreds of professionals.

The master key to sales conversations is stories: your stories and your future client's stories. You need to know what types of stories to tell — there are only seven — and how and when to tell them. That's why I've developed a framework for you, which I'll introduce in chapter 4.

Here are the seven stories (also summarised in appendix A):

HOOK stories — Stories to Connect
1. Your personal story
2. Key staff story
3. Company creation story

FIGHT stories — Stories to Differentiate
4. Insight stories
5. Success stories

LAND stories — Stories to Close the Deal
6. Values stories
7. Teaching stories

The different story types are characterised by the choice of *central character* and the story *purpose*. There's a story-type summary table in appendix B that you may wish to refer to as you read. And in appendix C, I provide a list of all the stories included throughout the book, so you can easily find examples of each type.

As a salesperson, your first and perennial challenge is how to make a meaningful connection with your prospective client to initiate a business opportunity. This is where storytelling first comes in, as you'll learn in Part 2, after we cover what a story really is in Part 1.

In the succeeding chapters I'll take you, step by step, through each of the seven story types, and how to use them to close more business than you ever thought possible. One story at a time.

Learn business storytelling and you'll have a multi-purpose master key to unlock all stages of the buying and selling cycle. Even better, you'll hold a magic tool, weaving its magic unseen, operating invisibly out of sight. With stories, you'll open up bigger opportunities, write better business and gain more satisfied customers. Why wouldn't you want to do that right now? So start reading — it won't take long.

Part 1

LURE

Story Fundamentals

In this part:

Why stories?

What are stories?

How to create them?

1. Why use stories?

Story is the fundamental instrument of thought. Rational
capacities depend upon it. It is our chief means of looking into
the future, or predicting, of planning, and of explaining.

Mark Turner, cognitive scientist, linguist and author

The Prague Play

March 1997. Stavanger, Norway. I've survived my first full
year as a quota-carrying salesperson. Phew! A challenging
ride that turned out way better than I had any right to
expect, thanks to some good old-fashioned luck! Selling,
I've discovered, is difficult and stressful. But now I've got a
different assignment. I'm one of the few technical experts
who know our new software platform, and I've been asked
to organise a software demonstration for a forum of 400
of our top customers, to be held in Prague in the Czech
Republic in a month's time. I'll have a one-hour time slot.

One hour! No software in the world is interesting
enough to hold a large audience's attention for an hour.
What to do?

An essential skill for sales success

Sustained sales success is achieved by demonstrating to future clients that your products and services will achieve outcomes they didn't think were possible. To do that you'll need to set a direction and change their minds. And the universal tool for mind changing is *storytelling*, as I'll explain in the chapters that follow.

But first, why must we change people's minds? Well, think about this. If buyers independently became aware of their need for your products and services, your role would become redundant. They'd simply ring up and ask for it or, more likely, select what they needed from your ecommerce website. Usually, though, the buyer won't appreciate how you can help them without a significant interaction with you. Their thinking doesn't include an understanding of how your solution can help them, or why your solution is better than your competitor's. To persuade them to buy from you, you'll literally have to change their minds.

It turns out that the best salespeople tell stories, whether or not they know they are doing it. And those stories do magical secret mind changing. Stories grab our attention, entertain us and change the way we think—all at the same time. But I didn't know that in 1997. Back to the software demonstration.

The new software platform to be demoed in Prague was the first to merge applications for five different oil and gas technical domains. The standard approach had been to get a technical expert from each discipline to demo each app individually. But my audience crossed all those disciplines. At any one time, four out of five people in the audience would not understand the demonstration. Then I had the whimsical idea of writing a play about an incident that required all five disciplines to interact with one another. I'd write parts for each of our five technical experts and get them to act them out.

'But I'm a Reservoir Engineer—I don't act!' declared Franz.

Others had similar reservations.

'We're gonna try it!' said I, pulling rank, and hoping like hell it would work.

For 50 minutes our audience of 400 managers, engineers, geologists, economists and geophysicists sat mesmerised while my team acted out a scenario from their business. No claims were made about the software, no feature dumps, no specifications. Just people they recognised going about their work in a way that had not been possible before this software was created.

'Any questions?' I asked tentatively.

Were there ever! For 45 minutes, through the scheduled coffee break and into the next scheduled event, the questions kept coming. No one left the hall. And our 'actors' stayed in character for every answer. It was amazing. The audience lived the story with our new software. They 'got' it, and they wanted it.

I have no memory of the script I wrote for Prague, but three years later I wrote another play for our Russian user-group forum in Sochi. I remember it featured Putin's dog, which got a good laugh. The Russians were just as involved in the play as the Europeans in Prague, and just as animated with their questions.

The clear lesson was that when it came to changing minds, a story was far more interesting and persuasive than assertions and opinions. Even an obviously made-up story. Since then I've learned that short, one- to three-minute true stories are just as effective and far easier to deliver.

When it comes to changing minds, stories are far more interesting and persuasive than assertions and opinions.

When I first noticed the impact of stories in sales, twenty years ago, I didn't understand *why* they were so effective. Even in recent years, when facilitating public and corporate story workshops, my stock explanation was limited to vague observations about how much we enjoyed stories as children and how, long before the invention of writing, early societies shared stories for social cohesion and survival. Story has been a means of transferring knowledge through the generations over tens of millennia. Now I understand that the importance of stories is fundamentally linked to the way our minds work. But more on that later.

The best salespeople use stories

The best salespeople are storytellers, and storytelling is an essential skill for salespeople. I know, these are big claims, and surely implausible ones? After all, library shelves are weighed down with books on sales training that don't even mention storytelling. In any case, who's to say who the best salespeople are? And if they do tell stories, how do we know they make a difference? Most sales conversations go unrecorded. Often great salespeople are unconscious storytellers. So we're talking about an activity that goes mostly unnoticed even by those who perform it. Hmm. That makes it difficult to pin down scientifically. Bear with me while I make my case.

Throughout this book you'll read about my own history with stories. In the beginning I used them unconsciously without noticing their effect, or at least not attributing it to the story. Then slowly, as I came to realise that stories have intrinsic power, I began to use them more intentionally. I still do so in my consulting practice. I've been fortunate to have worked with brilliant salespeople in many industries, and in our consulting practice we've sought a wide range of clients because variety is what makes our work interesting. I'd like to share the stories of the best salespeople in two of our newest client companies.

Matt and Joe's stories

We started with these companies in the second half of 2017. In each case there was never any doubt as to who the best salespeople were.

The first company specialises in commercial real estate. It's a 60-person firm whose founder and managing director, Matt, came to me with a specific problem. He'd built the company from a solo operation, but a recent illness meant that for some time he had been unable to fully engage in the business, and sales results had slipped.

I met Matt when his health was improving, and the first thing I noticed was his stories. He's one of a rare breed I call the 'stream of consciousness' storyteller. And these were not trivial stories. Matt's stories were designed to make a point. He dipped into his family history to tell me about his father and grandfather in the real estate business. He told me about being the top-selling salesperson in a large international real estate company before setting out on his own, and how he had built his business. He pointed out a property across the road and told me *its* story! The stories tumbled out, one after another, engaging and inspiring.

There's no doubt that Matt is his business's number one salesperson. Anyone in the organisation will tell you that. Matt is the model the sales team build themselves on. But even he hadn't noticed that his stories were a defining characteristic of his selling ability. So we set about teaching his sales team the company stories—and the team is doing well, becoming autonomous, with better morale and results, because we've cloned Matt's storytelling.

The second client is a software technology company. They specialise in digital transformation technology projects. I think of them as the elite SAS of software development. Crack programmers and technologists who drop in at the start of a digital transformation project and set everything up for success. They leave when the client can manage the situation on their own.

The founder and company co-owner, Joe, who understood the power of stories, engaged me to coach his team. Joe had built a highly technical organisation of about 140 people. When it came to sales, everyone in the company deferred to him. 'Joe is the salesperson,' they all told me. But Joe had reached his personal limit and knew that the business couldn't continue to grow while relying solely on his sales expertise.

One of my first tasks was to research the company story. Joe was too busy to be interviewed, so I met with five other people who 'knew' the story. But none of those I interviewed were storytellers, and I didn't think I was getting the essence of the story. When we ran our first story workshop Joe came along for the morning session. It was immediately obvious that it was Joe who had the stories. Like Matt, he was a stream of consciousness storyteller.

Joe told the story of starting his career as a technical expert rather than a salesperson but grudgingly agreeing to take on a sales role because the 'hired guns' were routinely falling. He became the best salesperson in the organisation. Then, when he came to realise there was a better, more ethical and effective way to sell and deliver software projects, he founded his own company. Like Matt, he told one enthralling story after another.

Two successful but completely different industries with two natural storytelling founders. I don't think it's a coincidence. We've just started delivering story training at Joe's company.

Now when I engage a new consulting client, I seek out the story-teller—there's often only one. These individuals are the keepers of the company's stories and they retell them naturally (often unconsciously). I love to work with sales teams in different situations, and I'll always seek out the storyteller who is responsible for most of the company's success. In my experience, where there are good, sustained sales results, there is always a storyteller at the centre of that success.

> **Where there are good, sustained sales results, there is always a storyteller at the centre of that success.**

How stories change our minds

Before I went into sales I was an engineer running subsurface surveys on oil rigs and then I specialised in rock physics. In the mid 1990s, I had a special project to test a new type of software called a 'neural network', which I was using for rock classification. There was a lot of hype around neural networks at the time but nothing like the hoopla they are getting now, because today, finally, they work! Back in the nineties, I spent a fruitless six months getting results I couldn't trust. Today's artificial deep neural networks are inspired by our brain's neocortex[1] and they are providing new insights into how our minds work and how they can be changed. Our brain wiring is still not well understood, but at the intersection of computer science and brain science incredible progress is being made.

I've been fascinated by how our brains work ever since, but Jeff Hawkins' 2004 book *On Intelligence* got me looking in more detail at the world's most complicated wiring diagram. Hawkins is an electrical engineer turned neuroscientist and AI researcher.

After making his fortune as the inventor of the PalmPilot, one of the world's first handheld computers and a precursor to today's smartphone, he founded his own neuroscience research centre.[2] Hawkins' (and my) fascination is not that of a psychologist who wants to understand human behaviour or of a medical neuroscientist who wants to treat disease. It is the fascination of the electrical engineer who wants to understand the wiring diagram. How does the bloody thing work? We want to understand the electrical engineering and information processing of memory, perception, cognition and creativity.

The explanation I'm going to give of how our minds change with story comes from science that is very new and still evolving. For those readers who would like to know more, I have provided both popular and scientific references throughout the text. If, on the other hand, I blow your mind, my apologies. Just move on to the next section.

The popular description of how our brain works is an evolutionary one.[3] According to this outdated model, our rational, 'thinking' new brain, called the neocortex, sits on top of our paleo-mammalian, emotional brain (our limbic system), which in turn sits on the 'reptilian' brain in our brainstem and spinal column. In this model, the rational and emotional brains vie for control with the emotional brain acting as 'first responder' for a slower mediating 'rational' brain.

In business we are expected to stick to rational thinking and keep a tight control on our emotions. Business should be 'unemotional', we are told. But this way of thinking about the brain *does not fit* the latest findings in neuroscience and information science. There is no 'rational brain', and there is no separate 'emotional brain' for managing emotions. Yes, the neocortex is the newest part of our brain in evolutionary terms, but it manages emotions and rational thinking and memory and planning and perception and action. All together.

Salespeople need to understand this because emotion and reason are both critically important in sales situations. They are the tools of our trade, and we must have an accurate sense of how they function. In this section, I draw heavily on the work of Professor of Psychology Lisa Feldman Barrett as described in her groundbreaking 2017 book *How Emotions Are Made*.[4] Bear with me.

Our neocortex, the large wrinkly outer layer of our brain, takes up about three-quarters of our brain volume. It is this part we must understand, because the neocortex synthesises information from all eight (not five!) of our senses (see figure 1.1). These senses are:

1. **Vision**—perception of the external world through light sensors in the eyes

2. **Hearing**—detection of sound from the world and from inside the body via the ears

3. **Smell**—detection of odorous molecules in the air through the nose

4. **Taste**—detection of molecules in the mouth

5. **Touch**—sensing pressure and temperature through skin contact

6. **Balance**—sensing the orientation of the head in space through structures in the inner ear (called the vestibular system)

7. **Body position**—sensing the relative position, orientation and movement of the body and its parts (called proprioception)

8. **Internal sense**—sensing the internal organs, including heart rate, thirst, hunger, pain, digestion, state of arousal, temperature, respiration, bowel and bladder (called interoception).

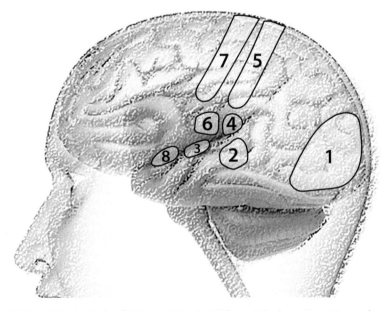

1. Vision; 2. Hearing; 3. Smell; 4. Taste; 5. Touch; 6. Balance; 7. Body position; 8. Internal sense

Figure 1.1: The eight internal and external senses mapped on the neocortex

The last sense, internal sense (interoception), is critical because our brain devotes considerable effort to keeping our body in balance through this sense—balancing our state of arousal and pleasant and unpleasant feelings, for example.

I'm sure you're wondering what this has to do with sales but hang in there, it's important. All our thoughts, knowledge and personality reside in the cortex. (I'll use cortex as a short form of neocortex from now on.) Our language, literature, music, arts, sports, scientific and emotional life are all encoded in the cortex. All the incredibly diverse abilities of human skill, imagination and creativity lie within that single organ, and all are processed, stored and operated in a similar way. That's because the cortex operates on a single common algorithm, which is called *sequence memory prediction*.[5]

Your cortex learns repeating patterns from your eight senses. From those patterns it builds one big model of your external and internal (body) environment and predicts what will happen next.

Then it enacts the prediction as action. All your conscious actions are in fact enacted predictions from the mental model in your cortex. The cortex is the 'first responder' in most situations because prediction is early warning. Anticipation is faster than stimulus–response.

What you 'see' with your eyes as you move around is not like a video image of the world—that's an illusion. The raw 'image' coming from your eyes is blurred and jittery. You focus on only the central part of your field of vision and your brain stitches these poor images together. So what you 'see' in your mind is a prediction of the world around you based on a mental model. That is how you can 'see' things with your eyes closed, as when you are planning or imagining something. Our brains spend a lot of time running the prediction model without reference to the outside world, that's what's happening when we daydream, plan or recollect the past. We update our world model when our predictions fail or when new experiences via our eight senses lead us towards change.

Emotions are an integral part of the model. We *construct* our emotions in our world model in the same way as we construct visual concepts such as 'chair' or the colour 'red', or abstract concepts such as 'money' and 'buyer'.

Imagine you are walking in the bush when you hear a rustle in the undergrowth on one side of the track. Out of the corner of your eye you see a shape and your mental model predicts 'snake', a concept that is stored together with an emotion called 'fear'. Fear, in turn, triggers an increase in your heart rate. You also feel an unpleasant clutch in the chest; you jump backwards and start to sweat. That's your internal body senses activated by the prediction. Your cortex created that fear by predicting it and sending a message to your body via your amygdala fear centre. Your cortex predicted the vision and sound of 'snake' and simultaneously predicted fear. Maybe when you look more closely and discover that the 'snake' is actually a stick, your heart calms down and your 'vision' is updated.

What if you had never seen a snake before and had never seen another person react to a snake in a way you conceptualised as fear? In that case, with no mental model of either 'snake' or 'fear of snake', you would not respond fearfully. The rustling sound would either pique your curiosity or you would choose to ignore it. You develop your mental model through experience.

You must experience repeating patterns from your eight senses to create and update your model of the world. Your experience may be direct or indirect, through someone else. If the snake was real and bit you, that direct experience would have triggered an update of your mental model of 'snake'—if you survived! Fortunately, we can learn indirectly from other people what a snake is and what to fear. If I tell you a story about seeing a snake, and describe or act out my fear, my story might arouse fear in you. A fear emotion from experiencing a story can induce a sweat and set your heart racing just as if it was you who encountered the snake.

Stories are a way to get others to share our experiences and to update their model of the world accordingly. That is how stories change minds. It's a salesperson's job to inject new thoughts into the mind of a buyer. To do that we must provide new experiences for our buyer, and stories can do that. Of course, your client's stories will also change your mind! You'll be a better salesperson for that; it's an important part of your sales education.

> **Stories are mind-changing tools. Your buyer's mind and your mind will grow with stories.**

The mind's natural language

Facts, figures and assertions are not our mind's natural language. They are hard for us to assimilate, because they are generally not in a sequence that starts us predicting. Stories unreel in a sequence and prompt us to predict what will happen next. So stories are a low-energy, low-effort way to pass on experiences and information.

Reading this book, you're in a fortunate position. You're learning something not many people know. If you can appreciate that there is an easy, natural way to communicate information, including the information that you are trustworthy and authoritative, and if you learn how to apply this understanding, then everything in sales becomes easier.

I'm a big fan of easy! But I'll work hard to create a system that makes life easier. I'm happy to put effort into preparing stories, because I've noticed that a two-minute story can do more persuasion work than a 60-minute presentation. Indeed, a short story can succeed where 60 minutes of energetic conversation fails completely. So why tell stories in sales? Because it will make your life easier and allow you to win more and better business.

I've found that anxiety is an experience shared by most salespeople. Anxiety about targets not yet reached, deals stalling, customers not responding, managers demanding results. Anxiety floating over a fear of failure. Few corporate roles create the consistent, perpetual pressure that sales roles do. Economic conditions change, business rivals become more competitive, but sales targets go in only one direction—up! Whether or not you've been successful in the past, you're always judged on your next performance. 'What have you done for me lately?' is the question every manager asks. By learning how to purposefully use stories in your sales process you'll have a tool that calms your anxiety. You'll be adaptable and successful despite changes in your business. That's how I have been able to move easily from industry to industry.

Stories avoid pushback

In his 1999 classic *The Secrets of Question Based Selling*, author Tom Freese describes the phenomenon of pushback—he calls it 'mismatch'—which occurs when someone asserts some unsupported facts and you mentally push back against these assertions. When we are presented with information in the format of opinion or assertion, there's a natural tendency to push back.

The way our minds work, we don't comfortably accept assertions if we can't easily find a pattern in them. If I say A, B, C, D and therefore E and F, you'll happily follow the sequence. But if I assert, 'Q is the 17th letter of the alphabet,' you may not be so sure. I created a doubt. Maybe you'll recite the alphabet to yourself to check? Someone may say (or think), 'Not in the Russian alphabet!' Your client may challenge your assertions but most will keep their resistance to themselves. They'll smile politely and nod, but they're not buying it, because assertions are not easy to process.

The mobile tower story

In 2009, when I was with Nokia, I had a meeting with the CTO of one of Malaysia's largest mobile network providers. I was accompanied to the meeting by one of our technical sales specialists.

As the meeting warmed up, I asked the CTO how many mobile base stations his company had deployed.

'Five thousand,' he responded.

Before I could ask my next question, my technical specialist jumped in with, 'No, you only have 4911!'

Gently kicking my technical guy under the table, I steered the conversation back to my next question.

What just happened? This was an example of pushback. It occurs, often as an automatic response, when a fact or assertion is delivered. In this case, the CTO delivered a 'fact' and my technical guy pushed back with his own 'adjusted fact'. Just to show off.

While we don't always verbalise it, we all push back when presented with 'facts'. One antidote to pushback that Tom Freese shares is to ask questions. It's true, you can't push back against a question but it's difficult to convey information with questions. You can also tell a story, because we also don't push back against stories, we relax into stories and listen to them. Stories and questions together are your anti-pushback tools.

Stories and questions are your anti-pushback tools.

Stories are memorable

The Springboard (Stephen Denning, 2001[6]) was one of the first textbooks on business storytelling. In the book, Denning relates his fruitless attempts to introduce the concept and practice of knowledge management in the World Bank in the 1990s. Denning's persuasion style had been to give elaborate PowerPoint presentations. When he overheard two World Bank case officers talking about containing a malaria outbreak in Zambia, he decided to include that story in his presentation. The impact of the story was immediate. Denning noticed that his audiences remembered the story and little else from his presentation. In the end, he ditched the PowerPoint presentation and just told the story! The Zambia story did the change work for him.

Indigenous Australians have a history of storytelling dating back at least 50,000 years. Their dreamtime stories teach each generation how to live, survive and thrive in the world's driest continent.

Recent academic studies[7] of stories from coastal tribes have found reliable descriptions of climate events that occurred about 10,000 years ago, at the end of the last ice age. *Ten thousand years.* That's a memorable story!

Hidden motives

American banker J.P. Morgan said, 'a man always has two reasons for doing anything: a good reason and the real reason'. Your potential customer doesn't always tell the truth (or the whole truth) *even when* they know and trust you. None of us do. It turns out that we have a rationalising brain, not a rational brain, and our true motives are often hidden, even from ourselves. Robin Hanson, author of *The Elephant in the Brain: Hidden Motives in Everyday Life* (2018)[8], has a useful metaphor: 'You are not the CEO of your brain. You are the press secretary.'

Hanson and co-author Kevin Simler show how motives such as desire for status, sexual partners or security are the true motives behind many of our decisions. The authors make the case that deception is a key survival skill in social tribes and that it makes sense to hide from ourselves our true motives — in order to deceive more successfully! In the words of George Contanza in *Seinfeld*, 'It's not a lie if you believe it.'[9] When people ask me why I'm writing a book, my 'press secretary' will respond with something altruistic along the lines of 'wanting to help others benefit and learn from my wide experience'. Other reasons are more egotistical, and commercial.

What chance do salespeople have of knowing what's going on if they are not getting truthful answers to their questions? The answer is in story *tending*. That means listening to the other person's story. One of the main reasons to tell a story is to prompt your client to tell their story. If the story you tell is honest and exposes your motives, you have a chance of receiving a matching story. Listening carefully for hidden motives in others' stories is crucial for understanding the political landscape of your customer's organisation. You'll learn how to use your story to trigger your client's story in Part 2 and how to untangle organisation politics with story in Part 4.

Stories solve the hard sales problems

There are just three fundamental problems common to every sales situation:

1. How to connect with buyers?

2. How to differentiate and show value?

3. How to get the deal closed?

Problem 1 is solved with hook stories: your personal story, company story and key staff stories. You'll learn about them in Part 2. Problem 2 is solved with fight stories: insight stories and success stories. They're explained in Part 3. And problem 3 is solved with land stories: values stories and teaching stories. Those are explored in Part 4.

The salespeople I work with are pretty good at researching prospect ideas. They can put together a target list of companies. It gets more problematic when they need to connect, gain trust and communicate an important new idea to someone they don't know. It's even harder to get that stranger to change and move out of their comfort zone. You can be lucky, catching someone who is a perfect fit for your solution at the perfect time. Everyone can have some luck and every sales process has its successes, but it's difficult to pull it off repeatedly and reliably.

Sales requires many other skills, but storytelling is foundational. If you have this skill, and the story map I'm going to give you, you'll be unstoppable.

Storytelling is valuable at all levels of the sales organisation, from the rawest recruit to the sales leaders, managing directors and CEOs. And it's a key skill that spans all industries and business types. You don't even need to learn all the story types to begin to derive benefits from storytelling; you can step your way through. Start with the hook stories and you'll soon enjoy benefits. Then work your way up through the fight and land story types to become a master storyteller. Once people see your results they'll want to know your secret.

The conventional wisdom

Some people consider stories 'unbusiness-like'. 'Just get to the point,' they say. 'Give me the facts and I'll make up my own mind.' Shawn Callahan, author of *Putting Stories to Work*,[10] started his business storytelling company, Anecdote,[11] in 2004. In those days, Shawn told me, you could hardly use the word 'story' in a business meeting without experiencing resistance. Today you hear it talked about often. In fact, the word 'story' is used in so many contexts it has come to be overused and often drained of meaning. However, once you have read the next chapter you're going to be absolutely confident about what a story is and isn't.

Many specific sales processes have been developed over the years—including 'Solution Selling', 'Value Selling', 'SPIN selling', and 'the Challenger Sale',[12] to name a few. In my view they are all incomplete, because none of them get to the heart of what the best salespeople do. A good example is question-based techniques like those espoused in Solution Selling and SPIN Selling. There's no doubt you need to ask intelligent questions in the right sequence, to listen carefully to the answers and to make appropriate responses. Questioning and listening are fundamental to the sales process. But questions in themselves are rarely persuasive. On their own, they cannot create new experiences, thoughts and ideas in your future customer's mind.

**Questions in themselves are rarely persuasive.
On their own, they cannot create new experiences,
thoughts and ideas in your future customer's mind.**

The conventional wisdom is that if you follow a specified (preferably branded) sales process, you'll be fine. But the idea of conventional wisdom in sales is problematic. The sales profession is awash with opinion but has generated very little science. It's messy and confusing, and it's difficult to get a clear view from the self-proclaimed experts. If you take ten B2B sales books at random you'll encounter a wide variety of conflicting opinions about how to sell.

Furthermore, you can have a poor sales process and still be successful. Buyers have to buy. That was my experience in my first year of selling. I was extremely lucky to win the biggest deal globally in my division that year. Winning that deal was not a validation of my sales process—I didn't have one! I was untrained and clueless. It's difficult to link cause and effect conclusively when there are so many variables and so much uncertainty. That's why sales leaders latch onto partial solutions.

Incomplete processes, competing opinions and the vagaries of luck—it all adds up to a minefield for new sales reps. They're given a target and don't really know how they're going to reach it. If they follow their company's established process, or the method plugged by some expert, with luck they may enjoy some success. The variety of selling situations is itself very wide, and what works in one context may not work in another. But storytelling works in *every* context. It isn't a complete sales process in itself. You still need to know your market, strategise, ask your buyers intelligent questions and listen with curiosity. But storytelling is the secret sauce for sustained sales success. It's the missing ingredient you've been looking for. With storytelling you can make success repeatable and even routine.

If you're the sales leader, manager or founder of your company, you probably have good stories though you may be using them unconsciously. Perhaps you feel frustrated because what you find easy, the people you employ find difficult. The problem here is they haven't experienced your stories. You can't scale your business if the good stories stay only in your mind.

To grow your business, the sales process must be less dependent on you. You must find a way to put your stories in the minds of your salespeople so they can replicate your success. Imagine coming to work to find all your salespeople selling like crazy, hauling in contracts. Gone is that sense of dread that if you are not there, the business will fall over.

2. What is a story exactly?

> *Story is atomic. It is perpetual energy and can power a city.*
> *Story is the one thing that can hold a human being's attention*
> *for hours. Nobody can look away from a good story.*
>
> Donald Miller, *Building a Story Brand*

It's important to understand exactly what a story is and is not. The definition may surprise you. Paradoxically it's both broader and narrower than most people think.

At its most basic, a story is a sequence of events within a recognisable framework. If there isn't a sequence of events, then it isn't a story—it's that simple. If it's not structured in a recognisable framework, it will be unintelligible. But most sequences of events are repetitive and routine, so we don't pay attention to them. To catch our attention a story must be interesting and unpredictable. What most interests humans is other humans, and usually stories have a main character, a person who plays a significant role in the sequence of events. Finally, we can tell stories to entertain, to educate and to persuade, but in business meetings we use stories to make a business point.

In this chapter we will examine the five elements of a successful business story. These elements are drawn from Shawn Callahan's excellent book *Putting Stories to Work*[1]:

1. There must be a sequence of events.

2. The story must fit a known framework.

3. It must be interesting and unpredictable.

4. It should turn on one main character.

5. It must make or illustrate a relevant business point.

A sequence of events

At the most general level, a story is a sequence of events. That's it. In a good story there is surprise, unpredictability and at least one interesting human character. Without a recognisable framework it will be confusing or even unintelligible. Without a business point it is simply entertainment. But here is the key thing: it's not a story *at all* if it doesn't contain a sequence of events.

In the previous chapter, I explained that our neocortex takes in information from our eight senses and synthesises it into a real-time model that we use to predict what will happen next and what to do next. The mechanism for creating the model is learning patterns that repeat. This is called Hebbian learning[2]: 'neurons that fire together wire together'. Sequences that repeat are learned. Once we have learned a simple sequence we use that learning to learn more complex sequences. Take this example.

A man walked into a bar.

To read that sentence on a page or screen, a part of your visual cortex processes the light signals from your eyes and recognises sequences of patterns. Areas in your visual cortex are dedicated to detecting the patterns that make up the letter A. In a similar way, the patterns of the other letters predict the words. The sequences of letters are recognised as words, the sequence of words as a sentence with meaning. You've no doubt seen this sequence of words many times, so you probably absorbed the entire sentence in one go. Now your mind is trying to predict what I'll write next. You're pretty confident it will be a joke. (A favourite variation: A horse walked into a bar. 'Why the long face?' the barman asked.)

We're good at noticing and remembering patterns in sequences because sequences are the information building blocks of the cortex. Switch on your car radio, and if it is playing a song you know, within three or four beats your cortex automatically predicts the sequence of notes that follow. You 'recognise' the song and sing along in your mind. This happens even if the song plays from a random starting point. It's a remarkable feat of memory. A song is a sequence of events in a framework and is therefore a type of story.

In computer memory we encode words and images as binary numbers. A computer 'remembers' with 100 percent fidelity what we feed into it, and each piece of data can be accessed directly. Our human memories aren't like that: we can often memorise complex sequences of events, but it's hard for us to remember unrelated facts unless we can organise them in a story sequence.

Imagine you had to memorise the sequence of a randomly shuffled pack of 52 playing cards or hundreds of random numbers. How would you do that? People who are good at memory games make up stories. For instance, they would assign each playing card an object, character or place so a story could be constructed from them. A character card visits a place card and sees or touches object cards there. For example, the redhead *queen of hearts* enters the *eight of clubs* library, sits in the *three of diamonds* desk chair and drinks from a *four of diamonds* glass. She moves from room to room in the house, with each room, and the objects it contains, represented by specific cards.

Using this story visualisation technique, amazing feats of memory are possible. At the time of writing, the world champion for 'one-hour cards' is Alex Mullen from the United States. Alex was able to recall the correct sequence of 1626 randomly shuffled playing cards after memorising them for one hour. That is 31 packs of cards. Anyone can perform this feat, though perhaps not to Alex's level, but all of us can use the language of stories to develop a high-fidelity memory.

As sequences of events, stories fit naturally into our brain sequence memory. The information in one story easily fits with the other stories in our mind—the sequence provides context. That is how everything is stored, in sequences. The alternative 'ask–pitch' conversation style doesn't provide context and takes much more effort to follow.

One reason we like music is that it too is a type of story, with overlapping sequences of sound patterns—rhythms and harmonies, that we try to predict. It might be less obvious, but visual images are also processed and memorised as sequences of events. Our eyes 'saccade'—move several times a second to put images together in sequences. Great works of art are patterns of shapes, colours, light and shade arranged so the eyes dance around the canvas and draw from it a memorable story. Sporting contests are stories too: an unpredictable sequence of events played out within the framework of the rules of the game and the playing field.

Our cortex uses our senses to identify patterns in the environment that repeat (sequences) and continually predicts what will happen next. Stories are high-order sequences. Brain food.

... in a framework

We can't easily process just any sequence of events. There is a hierarchical structure[3] in our cortex, an arrangement we've learned from childhood, and events need to fit within that framework. A sequence that violates that structure will be no more than so much confusing data until we make the effort to learn it. Here are two sequences:

2, 4, 6, 8,?

ɪe, ɗ, ±, ſ, ɟ, ?

The first sequence is in a framework you will understand (if you know numbers) and you have a good chance of predicting the next number. You probably don't recognise any framework for the second sequence apart from the question mark. So it's confusing. In a business meeting, there's no time for confusion, so you must adhere to accepted story structures.

I could create a piece of music using repeating patterns of notes, but if I don't follow the accepted conventions of rhythm, pitch and harmony of a specific music genre, my composition will be a cacophony. Works of art also need to fit a framework, to draw the eye through and across the work in a structured way. If we're unfamiliar with a new art direction, such as in abstract (non-representational) art, we may not recognise the work as art and may even find the work repulsive. That's because we haven't learned that framework yet.

... that are interesting and unpredictable

Your cortex is continuously recognising pattern sequences from the environment and using those patterns to predict what will happen next.[4] Mostly this is done subconsciously and automatically. You pay attention only when the prediction fails or becomes difficult. Have you ever driven your car on a familiar route, arrived at your destination, and wondered how you got there? At some level you simply stopped paying attention because your cortex was running a prediction it knew.

As another example, imagine approaching an escalator. You're very familiar with escalators, the grooved treads and rubber handrails, the rise and fall and speed of the steps. Your cortex predicts the sequence of motions needed and sends the necessary motor commands to your body. Your body movements are largely automatic and unconscious. But what if the escalator is stopped? Do you know that feeling? You almost fall over, because the prediction failed. Now you are paying attention! The story suddenly became very interesting!

When we listen to a story we 'picture' ourselves in the story, visualising what will happen next. But beyond just visualising what we would see, we predict with all eight senses: how we would move, what we would hear or smell, and most importantly, *how we would feel*. We predict our emotions as we listen to a story, as if we were the story's main character.

> **We predict our emotions as we listen to a story, as if we were the story's character.**

Good stories are inherently unpredictable. They keep us guessing and demand our attention. That's why we can sit for hours absorbed in a movie or a good book.

... that happen to a character

Most stories revolve around a central human character. Even when stories have non-human characters (think *Godzilla*, *Toy Story* or *Finding Nemo*), we give them human behaviours and motivations, because we care about humans and their interactions. Large parts of our frontal cortex are devoted to predicting what people around us are thinking and what they'll do next. It's a reasonable hypothesis that our large frontal cortex evolved as a result of the environmental pressures of surviving in social tribes.[5]

Reading or listening to a character's journey (sequence), we can imagine ourselves as that character and 'live' their experience. That's how the story creates an experience for the listener. Characters are crucial to stories, and selecting these characters is something we'll return to throughout this book.

Golfing with Frank

A few years ago I was in the clubhouse with my mate Frank after a round of golf. I was telling Frank about my decision to become a sales training consultant. There's not much that Frank doesn't know about selling. He's been in sales and sales management for thirty years.

'Sales training is a waste of time,' said Frank. 'The only useful thing is to listen to the trainer's war stories. That's all I ever remember.'

Precisely! That's how we learn—from the stories of other people's experiences. Frank and I have shared dozens of stories and learned much from each other while searching for our (mostly my) golf balls on our favourite links golf course.

Your story hero allows your listener to inhabit that character and experience the story themselves.

... and make a business point

Whenever you tell a story, there is a risk that someone will think you are wasting time, straying from the business in hand. You increase that risk if your story doesn't make a relevant business point. If your stories aren't relevant, your communication risks descending into mere gossip and banter, and that's no way to be taken seriously. Senior business people will not have time for you. By all means use humour and choose topical story subjects, but make sure you are delivering a message of value through your business stories. Sometimes an amusing story that goes down well in the pub simply doesn't work as a business story.

Skinning cats

A couple of years ago I ran a story workshop for a software company. We split about 50 of their salespeople and sales leaders into groups of five, and each group developed a success story. One of the stories was about selling to a charity organisation, the Royal Society for the Prevention of Cruelty to Animals. They were in the discovery phase with the charity when the client asked a question about how the implementation would be done. The sales guy responded spontaneously, 'There's more than one way to skin a cat!' Which prompted a deathly silence.

It's a funny story, a good in-house war story, but it doesn't make a business point, and it wouldn't resonate with future customers.

The simple story framework

Movies and novels can have complex narrative structures, but we'll be working with just two simple frameworks for our short oral business stories. The most common is the *simple story framework* (modified from Bosworth and Zoldan, 2012). Here the narrative arc consists of four elements or events:

1. **Setting.** By convention, the setting includes time and place markers. It flags the start of the story, sending the audience a subliminal signal that a story is beginning. Failing to start a story effectively is a common way to lose and confuse your audience. The setting is vital. It allows your audience to paint a mental picture and imagine themselves in the scene. 'That reminds me of when I was in Singapore at the trade show last year ...' Time and place markers are a universal signal that a *true* story is coming, so relax!

2. **Complications.** It's a boring story if nothing unexpected happens to the 'hero'. This is a critical aspect for an interesting story. Usually things go wrong or develop unpredictably. The complications create tension and suspense.

3. **Turning point.** Something happens that shows the hero a way out. Although vulnerability and failure are the grist of good stories, we have a strong preference for stories that end on a positive note. At the turning point the complications are being worked out and a way ahead identified.

4. **Resolution.** The complications have been resolved. The hero is transformed, having learned something of value, and the business point is made. Tension and suspense is resolved

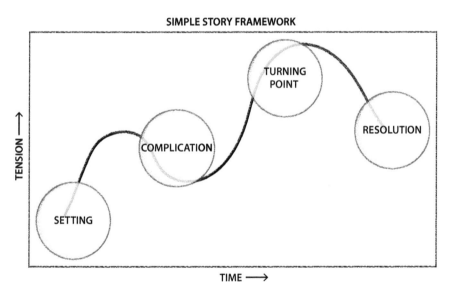

Figure 2.1: The simple story framework

In the simple story framework, the setting, complications, turning point and resolution unfold in sequence. The line in figure 2.1 represents the 'narrative arc'. To bring your story to life you need to describe each 'event' in some detail.

Like the simple story framework, the buying and selling process follows a sequence and is also a story. Both buyer and seller are engaging in a story (see figure 2.2). I use a fishing metaphor throughout this book to help you appreciate this sequence and remember the stories to use at each selling stage. You could apply the same metaphor for each individual story. At the setting stage you connect, relaxing them hypnotically into story listening mode. Then hook your fish. Then you fight to catch the fish. An angler doesn't know if the fish will take the bait or stay hooked, and therein lies the excitement of the hunt. The unpredictability of the fight is what keeps your audience's attention. The suspense is resolved when you land the fish. You've resolved the story and made your point. The story is over, the fish is caught—and set free!

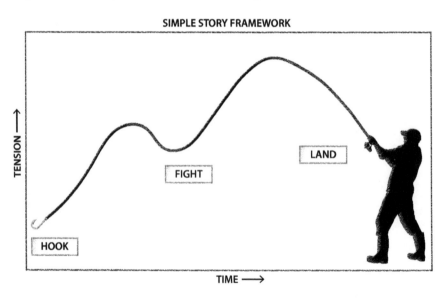

SIMPLE STORY FRAMEWORK

Figure 2.2: Fishing metaphor for story structure

Logic, mathematics and stories

By now you may be wondering where science, logic and mathematics fit in this brain model. Mathematicians and scientists have the same story-seeking brain as everyone else.

Logic and mathematics have their own structures and sequences. 'If this, and that, then it follows that' is a logic sequence. Arriving at a mathematical proof requires a setting (the starting point assumptions), a surprising event (a construction, a rearrangement, cancelling of terms) and a turning point to a proof. The proof is the point of the mathematical story.

For countless millennia pre-humans and humans used story to create and pass on culture. We just tweaked the story structure to develop the mathematics and logic that underpin the new culture of science and technology.

Storytelling is not the opposite of logical arguments, but it is the opposite of assertion and opinion. Logic and mathematics are delivered in a special type of story framework. We all understand the structure of stories, but while you need special training to understand the story structure of logic and mathematics, oral stories are universal.

Now we have a sense of what stories are, in the next chapter we'll look at how to put one together and then deliver it in a client meeting.

BUSINESS STORY ESSENTIALS	
A sequence of events	Otherwise it's **not a story**
In a story framework	Or its confusing
Unpredictable and surprising	Or your lose their attention
With a main character	Or they cannot 'live' the experience
Makes a business point	Or you're wasting their time

3. Tell me how it's done

People don't think in terms of information. They think
in terms of narratives. But while people focus on the
story itself, information comes along for the ride.

Jonah Berger, author and professor, Wharton School, Pennsylvania

Now that you understand why salespeople must tell stories and what a story is, let's get into the details of how you can construct your own stories. Even the best storytellers benefit from structure and technique. When I asked Matt (the real estate CEO in chapter 1) to review the story I wrote about him for this book, he told me to add the point that it wasn't until he understood the story structure from our training that he could help his team with their stories. As an aside, Matt was the best student in the training program.

There are three essential activities to finding and delivering a great story:

1. Interviewing and listening

2. Structuring

3. Practising.

When you master these three activities you'll be able to deliver any type of story. If you miss these steps, your stories are likely to miss the mark. Rushing into storytelling before the stories are well developed risks wasting your future client's time and missing out on the opportunities that a good story can bring.

We'll look at each of the three story-building activities in turn.

Interviewing and listening

Interviewing is a key activity and skill for story creation. Every sales story type requires interviews in the preparation stage. Even your personal story, as you'll discover in chapter 5. When you're interviewing someone to learn their story you need to get them talking. When they talk about something interesting, keep them there to get more details. A special kind of listening is required. You need to listen in a curious but non-judgemental way, using encouraging body language, facial expressions and gestures. Ask confirming questions to ensure you have understood and use leading questions ('Aha! Then what happened?') to move them on to other aspects of their story.

Through such active, participatory listening, you show you are a good listener, and you'll learn more too. If the other person is not using the language of story you've got two choices. You can either guess their meaning, filling in the blanks as best you can, and move on, or you can respond with confirming questions until you do understand. 'Help me understand that—how did that work?' 'Could you give me an example of that?' 'How did you feel when that happened?' You want their story but also to understand the emotions they experienced. Then you'll appreciate and remember their story, because you lived it too. Active listening, tending the story, is an intellectual exercise and an act of empathy that requires your full attention. Empathy is defined as the ability to understand and share another's feelings. That's a critical skill if you need to tell another's story and this style of interviewing is, by far, your best chance of being empathetic. That's because you directly ask about their feelings. Many people think they can infer feelings from body language and voice tone. Lisa Feldman Barrett calls this the two-thousand year (wrong) assumption.[1] Be aware also, that the skill of empathy is value-free; psychopaths can be empathetic. As with all sales skills, intent is critical. Compassion is the appropriate value response from empathetic interviewing.[2]

In our story workshops we start by pairing up and getting each student to interview the other to draw out their career story. The interviewer then presents the story to the group. Knowing you're going to be presenting someone's story in front of the group, you pay attention. You take notes and mentally rehearse. When a teacher announces that 50 percent of test questions will be based on today's lesson, the students listen with intent. The same level of attention is required when you interview someone to get their story.

Getting the essence of the story

A few years ago I was running a public storytelling work-shop in Melbourne with a diverse group of managers, sales leaders and professional services people. When we split into pairs to do the personal story interviews, I moved from group to group, listening in to check that everyone was managing okay.

I had paired a business founder CEO with Mariam, a Somali refugee advocate. When I approached, the CEO was interviewing her and I overheard him asking Mariam about her life in Australia. Mariam told him she had writ-ten a book and the CEO wanted to know about how she was marketing and pricing the book and other aspects of her business life settling in a new country.

Later, when the group reassembled, the CEO told Mariam's story. He told a good story about integrating into a new culture. He chose to start with her arrival in Australia as a refugee and the surprising fact that she was housed by the government in one of Melbourne's most expensive suburbs. But he missed important details that explain why Mariam is a refugee advocate. That story started in Africa.

I'd met Mariam for the first time a week before the workshop. Early in our conversation, when I complimented her on her English she told me that English is her fourth language. She'd left her native Somalia as a child to live in Kenya with her extended family because of the economic situation in Somalia. In Kenya she learned Swahili. As a girl, Mariam wasn't allowed to go to school, but she used to sneak into her brother's room to read his books. That's how she learned English. She learned to speak Arabic fluently after getting married and moving to the Middle East with her husband to live.

On a trip back to Somalia, Mariam got caught up in the civil war fighting and was forced to flee to the Kenyan coast. She spent two nights on a ship with other refugees sailing down the East African coast without food or water. When she arrived in Mombasa, the authorities were prepared to let her into the country because she had a Kenyan passport, but they refused entry for her children. Mariam stayed in a refugee camp on a football field, and because she spoke Swahili she became the spokesperson for the refugees.

You can see a video of Mariam telling her story at
master.mysevenstories.com/courses/sevenstories

This is an abbreviated version of Mariam's story, but do you now appreciate why Mariam does what she does? We need to interview in a way that lets the full story emerge, and personal experiences may be more critical to the story than career and business events.

The mechanics of story structure

Recall from the previous chapter the simple story framework. Each circle in the framework is an event that must be described.

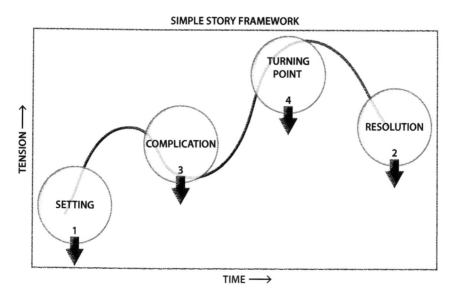

Figure 3.1: The circles represent story events that must be described.
The numbers indicate a good story **preparation** sequence.

Bosworth and Zoldan, in *What Great Salespeople Do*[3], recommend using coloured index cards for each event in the story—one colour for setting, one for complications, one for the turning point, one for the resolution and one for the business point. Start with the easy stuff—the setting and the business point. From there you can add the other parts of the story. The numbers in figure 3.1 indicate a good story preparation sequence. I've had great success with that technique in workshops. I've also had success with the single-page story template provided in appendix D. Participants' stories are more natural when they are guided by a few bullet points on a card, provided they describe the full event and don't just deliver it as bullets!

Most people find it easier to start by describing the beginning (setting) and the end (resolution). Then they fill in details about the complications and surprising events, and then they describe the turning point. Check that the story is making the intended business point. Finally, give the story a memorable name. That will help you recall it.

For stories that you experienced first-hand you may be able to finish here. When we tell stories that happened to us we naturally recall how we felt at the time, and the emotion comes out in our voice. For all other stories, we must think about the emotions that were experienced by the main character and check to see if those emotions are conveyed in our description and in any emotive words used. Great stories have emotional impact. We recognise them because we experience them viscerally. We predict how we will feel and our cortex sends the feeling via our internal body sense. That feeling in your stomach as you listen to a good story was made by your brain prediction.

An emotional journey

In our business story workshops, we ask participants to tell a story about a time 'when they helped' as a preparatory exercise when constructing a business success story. Most students tell business stories, but occasionally a memorable personal one will emerge.

Teaching swimming story

Nick, a marketing manager, told about taking his three-year-old daughter to the beach to teach her to swim. Nick took her into waist-deep, murky water, took her floatie arm bands off and kept close by as she attempted to swim.

Nick felt something brush against his leg. His first thought was that it was his daughter, but he could see it couldn't be her. He reached down into the water and pulled up a young, barely conscious boy from the sandy bottom.

Nick carried him, spluttering, ashore, whereupon the boy's mother came running up and exclaimed, 'Oh, there you are!' She grabbed the boy by the hand and led him quickly away before Nick could explain what had happened.

> You can see a video of Nick telling this story at
> *master.mysevenstories.com/courses/sevenstories*

I've retold this story in several workshops, and it never fails to draw gasps of emotion. But how is emotion evoked in this story? There are no emotional words, and neither Nick nor the mother's emotions are described, yet the story drips with emotion. Because it has situational emotion. When we envisage ourselves in Nick's situation we can imagine our emotions: 'murky water … felt something brush against his leg …' We're in the water with Nick and we can't predict what will happen. These words evoke emotions of foreboding and fear. Was it a shark? A box jellyfish? Seaweed? Then, '… led him quickly away before Nick could explain …' You're kidding me! The mother doesn't even know her child nearly drowned! We're exasperated, even outraged by this ending.

Nick's story leaves us hanging. It doesn't resolve neatly like a Hollywood movie, yet it is memorable and instructive.

The simple story framework of setting, complications, turning point and resolution has a sequence of emotions built into the structure, as shown in figure 3.2. This sequence is part of the story framework, an emotional progression that we learn and that may vary from culture to culture. Reviewing the emotions listed in figure 3.2, think about the language you could use to describe each of the four events in the structure. If the hero of the story has a strong desire for change, how do you describe that in the setting? Similarly, determine the primary emotion in other events and look for words and phrases that convey that emotion.

The most interesting stories have emotional contrast. We're taken on a journey through different emotions as well as events.

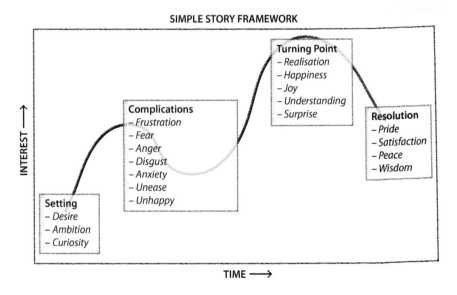

Figure 3.2: The emotional arc of the simple story framework

Figure 3.2 shows typical emotions that may be experienced at each stage of the story. You may not need to state that your character was feeling frustrated (for example) during the complications stage, because your description of what happened could suggest any emotional responses implicitly, just as in Nick's swimming story.

How long should stories be?

Your business stories should be as short as they can be while still making your business point. It's said that American author Ernest Hemingway once won a ten-dollar bet by writing a story in just six words. The story was:

'For sale, baby shoes, never worn.'

This story's origins remain unconfirmed, but there are some things I'd like to observe. First, it doesn't follow my framework! We, the readers, have to do all the work here, creating multiple story possibilities in our minds. I teach a story framework because we are *not* Ernest Hemingway! A genius is someone who can break out of the framework and still connect powerfully with the rest of us.

Another kind of genius is the stand-up comedian who can stretch a story out and keep an audience in stitches for an hour. In this book we won't be concerning ourselves with stories at either of these extremes. We're going to be telling everyday stories. Our shortest story is just 80 words long and takes twenty seconds to tell; the longest is 1000 words and takes five minutes. I can't get the five-minute story any shorter, but it is one of my favourites. It's the last story in this book. But for our purposes, a couple of minutes is a good mean to aim for, as it will fit easily into most business meetings.

A common comment in our story workshops is that 'some people don't like stories' and even a 20-second story would be too long for them. I used to believe that. I used to think it's better to avoid telling stories to driver-style CEOs or numbers-focused CFOs. Now I know those people also appreciate stories. Their brains are like everyone else's, but their time is precious, so your story must be tight and must make a relevant business point. The surprising truth about good stories is they work for everyone and they mostly do their work unnoticed.

The surprising truth about good stories is they work for everyone and they mostly do their work unnoticed.

Practising

When you have structured your story arc and worked on the description of these events to fit the emotional arc, it's time to practise and refine the story. There is no substitute for practice. I've found one of the best ways to practise is to record your story using a video messaging app like WhatsApp[4] and then listen to your delivery. Record and re-record until you're happy with it, then send it to a friend for feedback. Every repetition will make the story shorter, tighter and more interesting.

Stories are too important to fluff in front of your potential client, so practice is essential. In *Putting Stories to Work*, Shawn Callahan warns against writing out stories in full because we don't talk the way we write. That's good advice. Most of my clients practise with video message then upload the video to their corporate story library.

Another way to get started telling business stories is to join a public story workshop. That's not a plug for our workshops — we don't run many so you probably can't get into one of those. Search Eventbrite or a similar event website and you will find reputable companies offering story skill development. It doesn't really matter if the workshop you join focuses on leadership, change management, sales or some other business area. You could also join Toastmasters or a Rostrum club. The key is to experience co-creation of stories in a facilitated group.

One thing to look out for as you practise is voice tonality. It can make a huge difference to the power of your stories.

It's not just what you say ...

Recently I was facilitating a company creation story session with one of the sales teams I work with. I'd researched and written up their company story. When we practised the story in a group, I gave each of them the option of paraphrasing the story in their own words or reading my story. The ones who chose to read the story delivered it in a flat monotone. When I read it, it was animated by inflexion, pacing and the nuances of voice tone. The company's marketing manager said my version sounded like a completely different story.

Of course, I'd had the benefit of practising the story as I wrote it, but the reality is that written stories never sound natural when we read them, because we don't write the way we speak. If you record yourself telling the story, listen for your voice tone. Think about rising and falling inflexions, pauses and changes of volume.

Voice tone in storytelling

Voice tone in business communication, like storytelling, is an entire subject in itself. And like storytelling it is poorly understood because it operates at an unseen level, influencing conversation outcomes. In our Persuasive Voice Tone[5] training courses we teach salespeople how to employ the five 'selling' voice tones the best salespeople use, and how to avoid the five non-selling voice tones. As a memory aid, we equate each voice tone with an 'archetype' character.

The selling archetypes are:

- **The Authority**—a sharp, confident voice tone

- **The Friend**—a warm, easy, melodious voice tone

- **The Custodian**—a low-pitched, furtive, secretive tone

- **The Investigator**—a curious, questioning tone, used in exploratory conversation

- **The Negotiator**—a reasoning, persuasive tone, used when negotiating.

Only two of these tonalities—the Friend and the Custodian—are most suitable in storytelling contexts.

You can tap into the Friend tone by smiling and imagining the customer is your best friend. You'll naturally slow down and become more relaxed and outgoing.

To assume the persona of the Custodian you first raise your voice (loud), then lower it (soft) when you start relating the story.

'***Psst!*** Wanna hear a secret?'

'***You know*** ... I never really wanted to be a salesperson ...'

'***That's interesting*** ... Just the other day I was talking with a client just like you, and ...'

When you adopt a hushed tone, your audience leans in—they want to know the secret in your story.

What type of story to tell and when to tell it?

The seven key stories discussed in the next three parts work best at specific places in the buying and selling process (see figure 3.3). There are three steps to the buying process. First is the awareness of a need for change, then potential solutions are evaluated to see if the need can be satisfied, and finally a decision must be made on whether or not to take action.

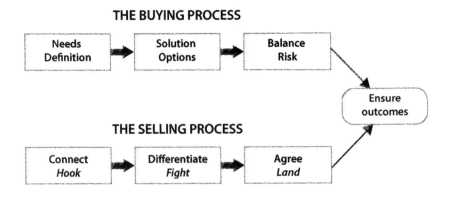

Figure 3.3: The buying and selling processes

In the selling process there are four steps:

1. **Prepare and collect stories.** Before you attempt to connect with prospective clients you have to know what you are selling, exactly what your buyer values and who your buyer type is. Without that information you have *no story* to engage your potential client. The seven stories prepare you for the challenge ahead.

2. **The Hook.** This is when you win the right to start the process. It means connecting in a way that gains your future client's trust, both in you as an authority and in the prospect of working with you. The best salespeople connect before their future clients even realise they have a need.

3. **The Fight.** In this phase you must persuade your future client that your solution, your company and you personally can and will satisfy their need and achieve the outcome they want. There will always be competing ideas in the buying organisation. The most powerful motivation will be to do nothing! Change necessarily involves risk, and since most people and companies are risk averse they are hard to change. The larger the organisation, the more entrenched the status quo. So you need to fight for your future client's mind space, and you'll need to be persuasive. Your fight stories will help your buyer to appreciate your unique offering.

4. **The Land.** In the final phase you'll land the deal. This means gaining internal agreement by overcoming typical barriers around risk, prioritisation and budget. Landing is the most challenging phase of the selling process, particularly for large deals worth millions. The larger the deal, the more decision makers are involved, and the greater the complexity for both your future client and your own company. It's also less likely that you'll be able to interact with them all personally, so you're going to need to rely on your champions within the

buying organisation. The landing stage of large deals is where the best salespeople shine, often using remote persuasion on people they don't even meet. If you want to be able to land large deals, storytelling is *the* crucial skill because it arms your sponsor with the story tools to get the decision made.

When you consistently deliver on these four phases you're doing your job and you'll excel as a salesperson.

Story planning and the story library

I grew up in Tasmania and was introduced to bushwalking by my father at a young age. By 15, I would set off with like-minded school friends on days-long bushwalking expeditions in the remote national parks of central and south-west Tasmania. One of our favourite diversions on these trips was joke competitions. Around a campfire or lying in the tent, we'd spend hours swapping jokes. The rules were simple: each took his turn and each joke had to be inspired by an aspect of the previous joke. The winner was either the last one standing or the one who cracked us up so badly we couldn't go on. The gorilla-and-the-salami-sausage joke comes vividly to mind.

I'm not saying you need to be good at jokes to tell good stories, but there are common elements. Good jokes rely on weird analogies. They're told, refined and retold—bad jokes becoming less so ... The best jokes are stories, sequences of events with a surprising, humorous twist. Often something in the preceding conversation triggers the story. Of course, the objective of business storytelling is to make a business point rather than to get a laugh, although sometimes you can have both.

It's okay to recall a joke when it's triggered by another joke, but hoping a good story will come to mind at the right time during a multi-million-dollar sale is a big risk to take. Better to think ahead about the story you'd like to tell. Many sales teams use a call planning process. This is a worksheet for salespeople to capture their meeting objectives and the topics they want to discuss in an upcoming client meeting. It's a discipline I tried to implement without much success when I was a sales manager, one of those good process ideas that peter out because the sales team resist it. A simple form of call planning that requires no process or ceremony is to ask two questions. First, the pre-call question, the one I ask my salespeople: 'What story will you tell in this meeting?' Then, in the post-call briefing: 'Did you tell your story?' You'll know if they did, because you'll get an excited description of how the story was received.

MANAGING WITH STORIES

Story Collection Process

| Learn to Identify Stories | Capture and Test New Stories | Trial Stories | Archive in a Story Library (Refresh) |

Implementation Process

Call Planning
Opportunity Planning
Account Planning

| Identify Communication Problem | Select Appropriate Story | Notice the Effect |

Figure 3.4: The sales leader's story management process

The best way to prepare is to create and preserve your stories in a 'story library', a searchable story archive that's accessible to everyone in the company. With this resource, you no longer need to rely on the conversation to trigger a story. What's more, the entire sales team has access to all the good stories. It's my experience that in any company only a few people have good sales stories to draw on.

By building up a story library, you multiply the success of your best salespeople.

In figure 3.4, along the top row you see the process of creating your sales team story library. The bottom row shows how to incorporate stories from the library in call, opportunity and account planning meetings with your team.

You can see what our story library looks like by visiting *stories. gifocus.com.au*. Most of our stories are written, but the fastest way to collect stories is to video them using a smartphone. No need for editing or a fancy recording setup, just make sure you have reasonable sound quality.

Story preparation checklist

✓ Start collecting stories.

✓ It's a business story *only if* there's a *sequence of events* happening to a *character* that are *unpredictable* and make a *business point*.

✓ Practise with video and share your stories in a library.

Part 2

HOOK

Making a Connection

In this part:

Personal stories

Key staff stories

Company stories

4. Who the hell are you?

*Vulnerability is the birthplace of connection and the path
to the feeling of worthiness. If it doesn't feel vulnerable,
the sharing is probably not constructive.*

Brené Brown, research professor, University of Houston

A member of your sales team comes back from a meeting with a prospective customer feeling very excited and upbeat. 'It was great! They love us!' A few days later he is a little less excited; a week after that he is not looking at all happy. The formerly friendly future client is not answering his calls. Why is that?

This experience is all too familiar to sales managers. The salesperson thought he had a positive, memorable meeting, but very soon his potential client has forgotten it ever took place, having become distracted by all the other things happening in their company. Despite all his investment in setting up the initial meeting, the salesperson can't now reconnect. This is a clue that the first step in the selling process, the connection, wasn't handled effectively.

The first problem in sales is connecting. It is a non-negotiable prerequisite of selling. You must connect effectively with a potential buyer or there will be no sale. When we meet someone for the first time they will have (mostly unstated) questions about us that need to be answered. Questions like: Can I trust you? Are you safe? Are you an authority who can help me?

The best kind of introduction to a stranger will be by someone they know and trust. Unfortunately, that often isn't possible. Even when we are introduced, important details about why we should be trusted will be missed, so it's up to us to demonstrate our integrity and authority. We can't just say, 'Trust me!' and 'I'm an authority on this.' That simply won't work. So how can we communicate that we're trustworthy, authoritative and worth listening to?

Many salespeople have a mistaken idea about trust in the buyer/seller relationship. Think about the times when you've made a high-stakes purchase and you'll appreciate that in such situations it can be hard to trust *anyone*, even yourself! All sorts of risks, real and imagined, chase one another around your mind. You worry you'll make a mistake that means you'll lose status or incur a financial penalty. In such a high-stress situation, when buyers don't even trust themselves, it's no surprise that salespeople are generally not trusted. There is no magic potion for lowering the stress of the transaction. There *is* a way to guide and support the buyer, but only from the position of a 'known friend'.

The journey to 'friendship' starts with sharing connection stories with your potential customer, 'hooking' each of you into liking and listening to what the other has to say. The three connection stories that you will learn to share are personal stories, key staff stories and company stories.

Before I talk about the three types of hook stories in detail, I need to emphasise that this is a two-step process. First, you tell your connection story, then prompt your future customer to tell you their story. This exchange of stories is absolutely critical. It's a rule of thumb that your connection as 'friends' can occur only when you have shared your personal stories.

Friendship can only occur when you have shared your personal stories.

Why are hook stories relevant today?

The mine safety story

When I joined a facility services company in 2012, I shifted from selling high-technology software to selling low-technology cleaning and catering services in an industry I knew nothing about. My new company was keen to break into one of the largest mining areas in Australia to provide camp management services to tens of thousands of workers in one of the world's largest mining companies.

When I arranged to meet the mining accommodation general manager (we'll call him Stephen), I was concerned about how to present myself. With zero knowledge of my new industry, my credentials were not compelling. I decided to be open about my lack of experience in facility services and tell the story of my career in the oil and gas industry, where, as in mining, worker safety was a consistent concern.

I met Stephen in the company's glitzy high-rise tower in Perth, Western Australia. After telling my story, I asked him to share his. He confided that he also did not feel qualified for his role. He had been in the army before moving into construction services. It turned out we shared a nomadic background as well as a concern that our respective companies were not managing worker safety adequately.

Stephen invited my company to bid for a tender to service their remote camps. Stephen provided me with important insight and guidance that helped us win that tender. In a formal process like that, it's unusual to receive coaching from the client. It will occur only when there is a significant level of trust. Our trust developed when we exchanged personal stories. We won that tender in a deal that delivered more than $150 million to my new company.

How does it look from the buyer's perspective? I've spent my career in large vendor companies, but occasionally a situation will arise where salespeople experience the corporate buying process first-hand.

David's tender story

When I was selling telecommunications services, one of our sales managers, David, told me about an occasion when he had to manage a 'request for quote' (RFQ) as part of a large deal we were bidding on. David had to score a competitive tender and decide on a subcontractor. Four companies were tendering for provision of equipment and services. David and a colleague, in typical analytical fashion, created a scoring matrix with score weights ascribed to all the things they felt were important to our company.

When they had tallied the results, they looked at each other and simultaneously declared, 'Well, we don't want *them* to win, do we?' So they changed the weighting factors in their decision table. Why did they do that? Because they wanted to advantage the company that connected best with them! This subconscious but important factor was missing from their scoring matrix.

The three hook stories

The three basic types of connection story are your personal story, key staff story and company creation story. I'm going to tell three stories that highlight the importance of each of these hook stories.

In subsequent chapters we'll look at each story type in more detail and explore how you can construct your own.

Personal stories

Although our company, Growth in Focus, is a sales consulting business, our founding managing director, Sue Findlay, doesn't consider herself a salesperson. She shies away from sales activities, preferring to leverage her technical expertise in procurement and buyer psychology, and to focus on winning tenders and grants.

The reluctant salesperson

Early in our company history, in 2015, I attended an industry conference in Melbourne, where I met Matt, the Perth-based managing director of an international geoscience technology company that I thought might be a good customer. I talked briefly with Matt at the conference and we agreed to continue the conversation when I was next in Perth. Unfortunately, each time I went to Perth, Matt was somewhere else in the world. It seemed we were destined never to meet.

After five attempts to schedule a meeting I emailed Matt and suggested he meet Perth-based Sue instead. His one-line reply was: 'OK I will meet her, but we're not buying anything.' Hardly a response to motivate an already nervous Sue.

I set up a meeting practice session with Sue and encouraged her to tell the story of why she co-founded Growth in Focus. It's the story of Sue's frustration with salespeople's inability to supply the critical intelligence she needs when helping companies to win tenders, such as the underlying reasons for the tender and the competitive situation.

Sue went to the meeting in Perth while I waited anxiously in Melbourne to hear how it went. A couple of hours later I got an excited phone call. 'Mike! We met, I told him my story and he said, "Welcome to my world! Let's go find a whiteboard" ...'

It was the start of a great business relationship. We've provided a range of services to Matt's company and trained his salespeople, an international team scattered across the globe.

We'll return to Sue's story in chapter 6.

Key staff stories

If you work with others, your colleagues are critically important to your sales success. Potential customers don't buy your products and services; they buy an outcome, and they rely on the expertise of your company to effect that outcome. By expertise, I mean the skills of specific individuals in your company, not the amorphous entity known as 'corporate expertise'.

The Voon Tat story

When I was working for Siemens, we sold a pre-paid mobile charging system to a telecommunications company for well over $20 million in a deal that took several months to negotiate and close. I was the salesperson.

When a deal is closed and celebrated, the salesperson usually moves straight on to the next opportunity, but I wanted to be sure the buyer was satisfied and I really wanted to know why our company had been selected, because we were not the frontrunner in the early stages of that deal. It was a competitive market, and the customer had many options of supplier to choose from. So why us?

When I met with the main decision maker we spent most of the meeting discussing the project implementation, which (thankfully) was going well. As the meeting drew to a close, I asked: 'Out of curiosity, why did you choose to go with us?'

The response was instantaneous: 'Voon Tat, your technical expert. He took the trouble to understand our technical requirements. And he showed us how we could achieve what we needed. *He* was the difference.'

The winning factor was our technical sales guy, not my brilliant salesmanship! Hmm, that was a blow to my ego.

Back in the office, I reflected on that response. When we decided to pursue the opportunity, I was concerned that our company didn't have technical expertise in Australia. Our main competitors, on the other hand, had supplied similar systems in Australia and had local experts. Fortunately, I had worked with Singapore-based Voon Tat before, so I knew his story and the quality of his work. I recalled telling the customer, 'We're bringing over our best technical expert to work on this,' then I told the story of how Voon Tat and I had worked together on a previous project and how good he was.

Pumping up our technical expert with a story probably made a difference, because the client was primed to accept him. Maybe the sales guy played a part after all?

It makes a huge difference if your potential customer knows about your key people early in the buying process, and stories about them are much more potent than assertions. You could insist your technical expert is highly qualified and brilliant, but everyone says those things, and in the end such opinions are barely heard. A story, on the other hand, is persuasive on an unconscious level. We love to hear stories, and telling stories about your key people early in an opportunity primes the engagement for a trusting partnership. Don't forget to prompt your customer's key people to tell their stories when you meet them, because you need to understand them too. When you have shared stories with your customer's team, you are no longer just a vendor.

Technical people in sales roles

A common issue for salespeople with a technical background is getting caught up in operational and support issues. That's one of the reasons why technical people fail in sales. Their heart is in the right place, they want to support their clients, but they end up neglecting their designated (sales) role. When I started in sales, I was the region specialist in one of the software systems we were selling. I remember incurring my sales manager's wrath when I solved a customer's technical problem on the spot in a client meeting. 'Mike, you never do that! You say, "Let me talk to our expert and I'll come back to you." Then go away, talk with yourself, and provide your solution to the support engineer.'

The key staff story is a brilliant solution to this problem. When you tell the story of your support manager or implementation specialist your customer is primed to accept them as the go-to authority. That frees you to move on to your next sales opportunity.

A key staff story primes your customer to accept your specialist as the go-to authority.

Company creation stories

The first time I noticed the power of stories in sales was when I was managing a sales team in Russia for Schlumberger in 2000.

The Schlumberger Russia story

Schlumberger was founded in 1926 by two French brothers, Conrad and Marcel Schlumberger, who had invented an oil well measurement—specifically, a technique to measure the variation of resistivity in oil wells. Oil has a high resistivity compared with water, which is what you normally encounter when you drill a hole in the ground. One of the first places to appreciate the value of this invention was the Soviet Union. The oil well 'logging' revolutionised the Soviet oil industry to the extent that a portrait of Conrad Schlumberger was hung in the Gubkin Institute in Moscow to recognise a pioneer of Soviet industry.

But the company suffered a huge setback in 1938, with Stalin's purge of oil industry intelligentsia. Schlumberger's assets were nationalised and the company was kicked out of Russia.[1] When the country was opened up again to western companies after the collapse of the Soviet Union in the mid 1990s, Schlumberger needed to decide whether to risk returning. The CEO was asked how much money he was willing to lose to re-enter the market. '$200 million' was his short answer.

Schlumberger set about investing in two of the top six Russian oil companies. They placed senior western executives in key roles, including head of production and chief financial officer. The results were startling. Using western techniques and technology, the two Russian oil companies doubled production in eighteen months while their competitors' production languished.

I love this story and told it many times in my meetings with Russian companies. When I heard it retold by my customers, I realised the story was doing persuasion work on its own. Its effect was remarkable and powerful. The power of company stories to capture attention and create a 'liking' for your company lies in the narrative journey. The trials and mistakes (complications) expose the vulnerability of the business process. Without the setback of Stalin's nationalisation, the story wouldn't have the same power. Today, Schlumberger has revenues of $35 billion, dominating the oil and gas services business and generating billions from its Russian business operations.

Each of the three hook story types—personal, key staff and company creation—is designed to make a specific type of connection with a future customer. It's a connection of 'liking' and 'authority'. Make this connection and they're hooked. Every aspect of the buying and selling process is easier from here on. Fail to connect and your chances are slim.

The hook stories make a connection of 'liking' and 'authority'. Make this connection and every aspect of the buying and selling process becomes easier.

I've introduced these story types separately, but it's possible and often preferable to merge two or more of them. I'll talk more about this in the next chapter. We'll also examine these story types in more detail so you can get started on building your own hook stories.

5. What makes a connection?

It's like everyone tells a story about themselves inside their
own head. Always. All the time. That story makes you
what you are. We build ourselves out of that story.

Patrick Rothfuss, *The Name of the Wind*

For most of our history humans lived in small groups, bands of
50 to 150 people. Encountering strangers was potentially dangerous—they might try to kill us. Over evolutionary time we developed social responses and behaviours to address this danger.

In *The World until Yesterday*, Anthropologist and bestselling
author Jared Diamond talks about the cultures of hunter-gatherer
and agricultural tribes that made contact with the modern world
only in the 20th century. He describes what happened in the Papua
New Guinea highlands when two strangers met on a jungle path.[1]
They would sit down and start asking about each other's relatives.
'Who do you know?' They would try to find a way to make a connection to their own tribal group and family. Without any common connections, the situation was dangerous and likely to end in
fighting until someone was killed.

Stranger danger

Of course, we've moved past killing strangers, yet we are still trying to determine whether any given engagement is safe or whether we should break it off. Today when we meet strangers, our minds are still attuned to that ancient behaviour, trying to see how we are connected and whether our contact is safe. We exchange stories about ourselves to find common ground. Part of our story is our tribe, or our company.

A prerequisite for being a friend is that you've exchanged stories in a common context. If you think about people who are your friends, you know their story and they know yours. To connect with a stranger (such as a new client) you need to tell a connection story. But that is only half of it. We tell our story so strangers will share theirs. The tricky part is to persuade your future customer to share their story.

You have to tell first, and here's why. They are unlikely to tell you their story unprompted, as typically strangers don't just start sharing their stories. If they do, their story is unlikely to be structured in a way that will lead to a 'fast friendship'. The content of connection stories is important. You must 'seed' the stranger's story with the content of your story, which is why you need to tell your story first.

You may have read admonitions from sales pundits against 'telling' in sales. As the mantras go, 'Selling is not telling!' and 'Question first. Listen then tell.' But those warnings are about a different type of telling. They are about starting a conversation by talking about your products and services. But with storytelling, if you tell your own story first and then prompt your future customer for theirs, you'll ensure a crucial exchange.

Your personal story must answer the unspoken questions the stranger has about you. *Why do you do what you do? Why are you here in front of me? Are you safe? Can I trust you? Are you an authority? Can I respect you?* Your objective is to answer those questions in a one- to three-minute story, then close with something like, 'What about you? Why do you do what you do?' By convention, the stranger will respond with a story of similar scope to yours. If you shared something personal, say about your children or your life partner, then you're likely to get something personal back, which is a fabulous thing! Exchanging personal details about the important people in your life is a great way to make friends quickly.

You'll read a version of my personal story in the next section. I include details about my partner, Megan, being eight months pregnant when we moved country for my first sales role. I also explain how lucky I was in my first year selling. You may not be comfortable sharing private details in a first meeting, but I'm going to coach you to share the true reason why you do what you do. That's what the stranger needs to hear; indeed, it's what you both need to hear to connect and build a business relationship. The best way to answer the buyer's safety questions is to do so in the context of a compelling story, because then you control the interaction.

The story you tell first should contain within it the reason you can be trusted, your honesty, your authority and your relevant experience. In response, you receive their story, which puts you in a privileged position. Once you've exchanged stories, you're on the way to being friends. You're on the fast track to building trust and rapport.

Telling personal stories is not well understood in sales. The main objective is not just to tell a personal connection story; it's to exchange personal stories and cease being strangers. It's the exchange that brings two people together to know and trust each other.

It's the story exchange that brings two people together to know and trust each other.

Once you have shared personal stories, you move on to sharing your tribe's or company's story along with key staff 'warrior' stories. The goal with each of these connection stories is to move further into the 'friend' category. To do that you need to exchange stories on three levels:

- **You.** Who are you and why do you do what you do (your personal story)?

- **Your tribe.** Who is your company? What is their purpose and how do they succeed (your company story)?

- **Your warriors.** Who are the champions in your company and how will they help this stranger (your key staff stories)?

Together these are your hook stories.

Is it time wasting?

Many salespeople, especially in western cultures, have the mistaken idea that 'meeting time' is precious and they need to get straight to the point by talking about their products and services. There are several problems with this approach. The first and most fundamental is that until you connect, any information you deliver will not be trusted. You're unlikely to be persuasive because you've missed the first critical step. First you need to connect and make 'friends', then what you say will be listened to and accepted. Of course, the stranger may listen politely even if you haven't shared stories, but their guard will be up.

I'll have more to say later about time perceptions in business meetings. For now I'll just say it's never wasting time to make a good connection with your future client.

Connecting the dots

Connection stories are stories about you, your people and your company. They communicate how you got where you are and why you do what you do. It's important to have a narrative thread running through your stories, with one event flowing naturally to the next. They must also be realistic, conveying the obstacles and vulnerabilities of the journey. And they must be true stories. A story that shows a steady linear progression to fabulous success is not believable, interesting or relatable. You need to include things that went wrong and personal stumbles so the 'stranger' can relate at a human level. By all means end the story on a positive note, but the ups and downs of your journey are what give your future customer the confidence to tell their own story.

As a salesperson, your first hook story is your own personal story, but your key staff stories are critical too, and in a way they are easier to tell. Your personal story needs to be humble and self-effacing, or at least you need to avoid bragging about your experience and performance. But when you tell the story of an important player in your team, you can afford to be complimentary and to build them up.

The third type of hook story is your company creation story. Here you are representing the organisation rather than yourself. Your future customer will want to know who this company is, what they do and what they can offer. If the company is well known, is their idea of it favourable or even accurate?

You need to convey why what your company does is important and relevant. The time-honoured way of doing this is to list your company's achievements. 'We've been in business since ... We have a staff of ... We're number one at ... and we're great at ...' This type of approach does not connect. Worse, it invites pushback and rejection. You're hitting them with information they're likely to refute because it is presented as assertion and opinion. It's in the wrong format. You need to communicate your company's credentials in the format your client is most open to: you need to tell your company creation story.

Many of the business owners and sales leaders I work with are natural storytellers. Their stories spill out spontaneously, stream of consciousness style, one after another, like the joker holding the floor in the pub. These stories have an impact, but they're even more powerful when delivered strategically, consciously and succinctly. We'll learn how in the next chapter.

We've discovered that a few short, high-quality stories are much more effective than a great cascade of stories, and that they're also much easier to teach a sales team.

Mike Bosworth is famous in B2B sales training circles through his influential 1995 book, *Solution Selling*, which is essentially a questioning skills manual. Solution selling became the reference training method for many corporations, including Nokia when I was working for them in the late 2000s. We trained all our salespeople in Bosworth's method, which specified the type and sequence of questions to ask in a sales conversation. There were nine boxes of question types and you had to know where you were within the boxes during the customer conversation.

I was a big fan of *Solution Selling* long before I joined Nokia, but I struggled to teach my people his questioning technique because it's complicated. It's one of those techniques you're likely to get worse at before you get better, because you are forever trying to think of the next question type rather than listening to your customer's responses. *Solution Selling* is also silent on the rapport-building and the persuasive power of storytelling

In 2012, Bosworth addressed the rapport issue by teaming with Ben Zoldan to write *What Great Salespeople Do*, a wonderful book on storytelling. Curiously, the book argues against the solutions selling approach and instead teaches storytelling as a sales conversation methodology. Central in the book is a story Ben tells of when he worked with Bosworth as a solutions selling sales trainer, which I'll paraphrase here.

The sales trainer's nightmare

At the end of a training course for a corporation, a student invited Ben to observe him in a client meeting that was due to start in the same building. (This situation would have filled someone like me, who has been a sales manager and sales trainer, with deep foreboding.) Ben accepted. When they stepped into the meeting room they were surprised to find the student's CEO chatting with the visiting client team. *Oh well,* Ben thought, *this is an opportunity for the CEO to see the results of the training program we've been delivering.*

The student duly launched into a series of questions following the questioning framework he'd been taught by Ben. The lead client leant back, arms folded and refused to play along. While the client became more and more frustrated with the line of questioning, the student persisted. Concerned about this poor reflection on his training method, Ben jumped in to retrieve the situation, but his questions made the client even more unresponsive.

Finally the CEO of the student's company leant forward and said, 'You know, this reminds me of when I was working at …' and proceeded to tell a story about a situation similar to the visiting company's. As soon as that story was finished, the client leader related a similar experience. Then they were trading stories about their families … and the meeting got back on track.

From this and similar experiences, Bosworth and Zoldan were persuaded that the solutions selling method didn't work, and they discarded it in favour of a storytelling approach. My own view is that questioning techniques are not invalidated by experiences like Ben's. He and his student simply got the sequence wrong.

The exchange of stories has to come first. After that transaction you can relax and safely adopt a questioning technique—and tell some more stories. Questioning before trust is established doesn't work.

Building rapport

The modern B2B sales process is said to have been invented by John Henry Patterson in 1893[2], when he was working for National Cash Register (now NCR). Patterson codified the first professional B2B sales process, known as *The Primer*, by inscribing it in a twelve-page notebook his brother had given him. The Primer covered every aspect of the sales conversation 'performance'. NCR salespeople were taught to establish rapport 'as the Primer advised, by studying the prospect and gaining his confidence'.[3] First they would notice some particular in the person's office or appearance, maybe a photograph or ornament on their desk or a painting on the wall. Then they would ask about that and pretend to be fascinated by the person's response. The method probably enjoyed some success, but it was essentially manipulative and it's now seen for what it was—fake and inauthentic.

Today this sort of warm-up is not received well in most business settings. People are too busy and you're not answering the fundamental unspoken questions: *Who are you? Why are you here? What's your intent? And why should I trust you?* If you're not addressing those questions, if you're talking about football or golf or some other unconnected topic, it's likely to be viewed as time wasting.

Where I live in Melbourne, Australia, many companies think hiring a former Australian Rules footballer is a good idea for sales roles. A well-known sporting person can easily start a conversation with people who know football, but their experience is based on sporting ability that more than likely has no bearing on the client's business, so how can they help? The idea that the ability to share a conversation on *any* subject is the key to rapport is wrong, because such discussions don't address the buyer's primary safety concerns about your trustworthiness. From the seller's perspective, this approach is also less likely to lead to a story exchange that will form the basis for a 'friendship'. Of course, ex-footballers can be great salespeople—I know many who are—but making a connection only on the strength of hero worship is not sufficient.

Why do people still follow a traditional approach?

That first business meeting with someone you don't know can be an awkward experience. You asked for the meeting and it's your job to start the conversation. It doesn't feel right (and it *isn't* right) to jump straight to business, but what else can you talk about? Just as when meeting someone for the first time at a party, you look for things you have in common.

It's often said that good salespeople are easy conversationalists, that they have the 'gift of the gab'. But most business people are impatient. They don't want to waste time on small talk; they want to know what you're going to do for them. Now.

Salespeople have learned to drop the conversation about the family photo on their customer's desk, but if they jump straight to business they've missed a crucial step. A common misconception is that if you tell a story about yourself, you're time wasting again. That's not true. The most interesting things in the room are not the furnishings or the latest sports news. They are the two humans who don't yet know each other. Let's talk about that.

Personal stories get attention. We are naturally drawn to stories, but especially personal ones, because they're unpredictable and we want to learn from them. Could our life have been like this person's? How did they survive and succeed? Chatting about last Saturday's game may be entertaining—although there's a good chance that at least one party is only feigning interest—but football chat doesn't progress your business relationship. When you tell a relevant story that has an unpredictable sequence of events and human interest, people take notice. They listen, and they don't even notice time passing.

What's in a personal story?

That's a good question. No one has time for your whole life history. Personal stories are vignettes, snapshots of times in your career that illustrate who you are and why you do what you do. When I tell my story as a sales trainer and business consultant, I need to explain how I got into sales, why I want to help sales teams and how I can help. I graduated from university as an engineer. At that time I had no interest in sales. In fact, I saw sales as a dark, manipulative art. So here's my short story.

Mike's story

In 1996 I was working in the United Kingdom as a rock physicist. I would analyse data from oil and gas wells and interpret the rock and fluid type. My company had created new software for geoscientists and wanted to sell it to oil and gas companies. One day I was called into my manager's office and told, 'Mike, there's this opportunity for you that's going to be great for your career. We want to send you to Norway to sell our software.'

'Whoa! Norway, excellent! ... Sell software? I don't think so ... that's not me.' It was a dilemma. At the time Megan was eight months pregnant so moving country should have been out of the question, but she's more adventurous than I am! We ended up flying on the last possible day the airline would accept her. We landed in Stavanger heavily pregnant and with a two-year-old toddler. When

Megan was giving birth a month later, I was busy on a very early model mobile phone, trying to be a salesperson.

I received good sales training, but I didn't have much idea of what I was doing. In that first year, though, I closed the biggest deal in our company division, and it happened purely by accident! I was, as I now appreciate, in exactly the right place at the right time. The deal was done because of a remarkable 'mobiliser' in the client organisation. However, as often happens with salespeople, I took that good fortune as evidence of my own talent. I thought I was good at sales. I stayed selling and ended up in sales leadership, managing sales teams in Russia and throughout Europe. In a booming market, I had considerable success.

When it was time to come home, we decided to live in Melbourne, where there was no possibility of work in the oil and gas industry. I worried I might not be able to find work. Do you know the feeling? Lying awake, bathed in sweat, worrying about never finding work again. As it turned out, I told a good story in a job interview and managed to get a role in the telecoms industry selling mobile networks to telecommunication carriers. I used to joke that I was perfect for the role, apart from the minor impediments of zero knowledge about my products and services, my industry or my customer. When I learned the trick of changing industries, I story-told my way through four more industry transitions, always in sales roles.

Throughout that time, as a sales leader but still an engineer at heart, I wanted to understand how we sell. What's the best technique? Who are the best salespeople? What makes them good? I had a common experience across diverse industries: I had sat next to salespeople in client meetings as they routinely said the wrong thing, failing to connect, to differentiate, to close.

I noticed that the best salespeople told stories that made me think, and I came to understand that this was the answer. It has consistently worked for me, which is why I've found success in several industries, and I believe it's what most salespeople need to learn. In 2014 I decided to go out on my own as a consultant, to see if I could make a difference for sales teams by teaching them storytelling.

> You can see a video of Mike telling his story at
> *master.mysevenstories.com/courses/sevenstories*

That's an example of a personal story. It's quite long, and I wouldn't always tell it with so much detail. I might tell different parts of the story depending on the context. There are three turning points in my story: my conversion from engineer to salesperson; my return, jobless, to Melbourne; and my decision to become a business consultant.

You can visualise the story as the simple framework with two complication cycles, as shown in figure 5.1. Each complication event is a mini-story in itself and could be told independently.

You can select from a pallet of personal story 'vignettes'. Choose one or two career events that have a story trajectory and that answer the question of why you do what you do and why you're sitting here, in front of this stranger.

To develop your personal story, I recommend you have someone interview you. I've found most people are not good at identifying what's interesting in their own story. They know the story so well that to them it's just not that interesting. (Interviewing skills are also really useful for eliciting key staff stories, as we'll discuss in the next chapter.)

Other people will find different things about you interesting. How did you get into your field? What did you study at university? What made you want to do that? What happened to make that happen? These are the sorts of questions the other person will have in mind. They won't ask you, but they will be curious, and you can answer at least some of them in your story. If you choose to seed your story with personal references, like my mentioning that my partner was pregnant when we moved to Norway, then you are likely to trigger personal disclosures in your client's story.

You may prefer not to share personal aspects of your story. Be aware, though, that a personal connection is stronger than a business-only connection. When I talk of my experience of being with salespeople when they're saying the wrong thing, and my conviction that there has to be a better way to connect, and to do so more successfully, I'm conveying my intent and my purpose. That's why I do what I do.

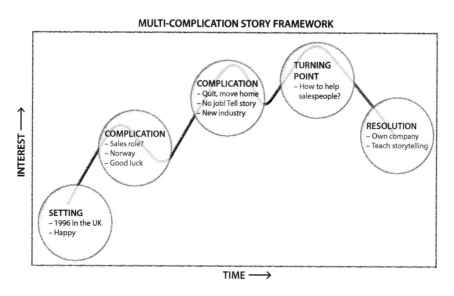

Figure 5.1: The story framework for Mike's personal story

Why is connecting a hook?

You may be thinking 'hook' sounds a bit aggressive and manipulative. Why do I call them hook stories? As we've discussed, the fishing analogy works on several levels. You have products and services and an assumed market for them. You need to find a way to get in front of people who can use those products and services. Your story is the lure and if you hook properly and make a good connection, the rest of the sales process will be much easier. Yes, there may be struggles along the way, but you've got a good chance of going the full distance.

Without a secure connection, you'll get some false bites but the fish will always break free. When you hook properly, you've started a process that can lead to new business. You won't land them all. Sometimes the fish will jump off the hook; sometimes your line will break because your position isn't strong enough, but with a proper hook you give yourself a chance—you're in the game. You cast your connection stories near the fish. In the exchange of stories your client decides whether or not to bite. If they trust your intent and believe you have sufficient authority to help them, they may allow themselves to be hooked.

I know the analogy breaks down when you consider it from a real fish's point of view. After all, a fish generally doesn't get a good deal when you catch it, but in a business deal both sides must benefit. When it comes to landing the deal, it must be cause for celebration by both buyer and seller.

To stretch the analogy, marketing is like setting a fishing net, going away and hoping you'll make a good haul when you pull it in later. Selling is more one-on-one intentional. I aim to catch a particular fish. Based on my own research, I'm convinced our business relationship will create mutual benefit, so I cast my line. The salesperson who comes back from a meeting excited by the prospect of a deal may have got a bite but didn't hook their fish. It's important to understand that to be successful, you need a connection that hooks deep.

That my sales career has spanned multiple industries is unusual. It means I have great connections around the world in diverse industries, and many of them are still friends. If I travel to a place where I've done business in the past, I like to catch up with past clients even though I no longer work in their industry. The story exchange creates lifelong friendship.

In the next chapter, I'm going to show you all that goes into a connection story, and how to develop your own diverse connection stories so you have a range to choose from, which is where the creative part comes in.

6. Instant rapport!

It's from those true connections where I finally feel understood.

Corin, Poet and blogger

If people tend to be wary in their first interactions with strangers, this is especially so when the strangers are salespeople, who must carry the baggage of past poor selling practices. Sharing stories is a way to break through this resistance. Salespeople are trained to ask questions. We have a question for every situation, but there is a huge difference between the answers you receive when the buyer feels safe and the ones you'll get when their guard is up. If you don't first make a connection through story, you will keep blundering along, an average salesperson at best. You'll wonder how that select few, as if by magic, connect so easily with potential buyers to create unexpected business.

Why is connection so important now?

In today's frenetic business environment, there is a huge premium on time. An important aspect of business is lost if we fail to appreciate the central role of human connection when doing business.

The danger is we will end up interacting in a shallow way, which means business is unlikely to proceed, or it will fail through misunderstanding.

The technological trend is to reduce everything to an algorithm to save time and reduce human connection — check these boxes; if you have that problem, then this is the solution. According to a famous statistic in sales guru–speak, modern buyers use the internet to traverse 57 percent (such a precise number!) of their buying journey unassisted. They interact with a buying organisation only when they have almost made up their mind. I don't buy it. I think that's untrue on many levels.

A vendor organisation has information, experience and knowhow that the buying organisation can never have; if they had the same information and skills, they would be in the same business. The vendor has insights and knowledge from all their other client situations. It's impossible to purchase complex products and services without a deep interaction and connection with experts, and those experts are predominantly in the vending organisation.

Platforms such as eBay allow you to educate yourself before making simple online transactions. It's neither possible nor desirable to approach complex B2B sales that way. 'Buyer in control' is not a helpful idea in this context. Your company and your potential clients each draw on deep experience and expertise. The only way to do complex business is to understand each other at a deep level, and that requires that human beings who trust each other interact as equals. The hook stories we discussed in the previous chapters get you to that level of interaction.

Buyers delude themselves if they imagine they're negotiating 57 percent of the buying journey on their own. They don't even know what they don't know. In many cases they don't even know it's a process they should start. Sellers delude themselves if they think they can just ask textbook sales questions and trust the answer from someone with whom they have yet to create a connection.

Lowering the barrier through the exchange of personal stories gets you to a position of safety and trust, but it doesn't mean you understand your potential client's situation. You need to understand their specific objectives, challenges and opportunities, and also the financial impact of resolving those challenges, achieving those objectives and taking advantage of those opportunities. Finally, you need to understand what constraints exist within their organisation and market. These are things you absolutely need to know before you propose anything. What is required is a consultative approach, with refined questioning and listening skills, but that's outside the scope of this book. (We teach questioning and listening in our Story Meetings coached online training courses.[1]) Until you're trusted, though, you won't get to a place where you can ask those questions and be sure you're getting honest answers.

Keep in mind that the trust you have built is easily blown! Your line is broken the instant you propose something that's not a good fit, and you blow it all away. It's a trust killer. I see it happen all the time. What Mike Bosworth calls 'premature elaboration'[2] is the number one affliction of salespeople everywhere.

Let's return to the three hook connection stories:

- your personal story

- a key staff member story

- your company creation story.

More on personal stories

I told my own personal story in the previous chapter. It took me longer to develop that story than it should have because I did it on my own. I now know that it's better to collaborate on this project, because we are often not a good judge of what is interesting about ourselves. We are so familiar with our own story that it's not interesting or even quite real to us. We have a distorted idea of what is interesting in our story because we don't see ourselves as others see us. What we experience and relate to is the mental model we have of ourselves.

Tabatha's story

When I was preparing to run my first public story workshop some years ago, I worked with Tabatha, a friend who was starting her own business in change management consulting. Tabatha and I had worked together at Nokia, and she had tremendous experience organising and managing large change projects affecting tens of thousands of people. Now she was starting out on her own I encouraged her to work on her personal story.

Tabatha is a pragmatic, logical person and the idea of telling a personal story didn't fit well with her at first, but I was insistent. I offered to interview her to help her get started. Tabatha told me about her first job working in local government, managing projects with complex stakeholder groups. She needed to mediate and manage resource squabbles involving local community groups, councils, state governments and the federal government. Then she told me about her international career and experience with multinational companies.

I sat back and reflected on this career story. Somehow it didn't seem complete to me.

'What got you into this line of work? What did you study?"

It turns out she had studied anthropology at university.

'You don't think that's relevant?'

Tabatha hadn't thought her education background was interesting at all, but it was fabulous training for someone involved in changing human organisational behaviour. She now has 'Corporate Anthropologist' on her business card!

A couple of days after I helped Tabatha with her personal story she rang to tell me about a phone call she had just made to a potential business partner in London.

'I decided to tell her my story, and you wouldn't believe her response! She told me *her* life story, including things I think even her husband doesn't know! It's like we're life-long friends!'

You can see a video of Tabatha telling her story at
master.mysevenstories.com/courses/sevenstories

When we define our own image of ourselves, we are in danger of losing sight of what others see as interesting, true and authentic about us. Also, we tend not to talk about things that went wrong and times when we were vulnerable, but that's the good stuff! Sharing the highs and lows make the stories real and enable a more authentic exchange. Just as with company stories, the personal story that goes, 'I was born a genius, was brilliant at school and was immediately successful in my business, which has grown exponentially …' is neither believable nor relatable.

Your personal story should be no longer than two to three minutes, otherwise it will seem like you are only interested in yourself. So, what to include and what to leave out? In two to three minutes you can touch on only three or four specific events. The older and more experienced you are, the more material you have to choose from. You must be very selective, because stories are killed by generalisation and commentary. A story that degenerates into bullet points and exposition ceases to be a story and fails.

Focus on the turning-point events in your life and career: Why did you choose your field of study? How did you get into this industry? What led you to the role you're in now? What was a major turning point in your career? Were there other paths you could have chosen? What do you most like about your job and why? Don't be afraid to include false starts and failures, because these are the events that make your story interesting and engage your client's emotions.

The most innovative business genius on the planet today may be Elon Musk. Go to YouTube and listen to Elon talking about the times when his businesses nearly failed and he was down to his last dollar. It has happened several times. He also talks freely about how his personal life went off the rails. There aren't many who can match Musk for business innovation, yet his story is human and relatable. He doesn't portray himself as Superman, and that's a strength.

Let's look at another personal story. I began this part of the book by introducing Sue, my business partner, who used her personal story to engage with one of our first clients. Here is the story Sue told.

Sue's story

I trained and worked as a medical scientist after university. I travelled to Saudi Arabia and worked with my husband in a government hospital there. I also worked in Tasmania. The travel was great, but after a few years in a lab coat I needed a change, so I took a role in government procurement and became responsible for procuring tens of millions of dollars' worth of telecommunications products and services each year.

During this time I met many salespeople and read a great many tender responses. I have to say, the vast majority of them absolutely failed to communicate the important aspects of the supplier's business that I needed to know. So in 2003 I started my own tender assistance business, helping companies all over Australia to win tenders and grants.

I had a very high success rate, but my biggest frustration was the companies that came to me for tender assistance (normally at the last minute) without the critical information I needed to help them win. Things like the customer's real reason for tendering, the personal and business objectives of the key decision makers and the competitive landscape—basic opportunity information that the sales team should have collected. Without that critical information, there was no way to craft a winning tender and I had to turn down the work.

The problem was, and still is, substandard sales work before the tender release. I thought back to the stream of salespeople who traipsed in and out of my office each week when I was head of procurement. I could count on one hand the ones I could trust to really help me. No wonder they struggled with tenders. That's why Growth in Focus was created. It's a sales consultancy designed to complement the bidding consulting business. We want to lift the professionalism and competency of salespeople, and since 2014 that's what we've been doing!

You can see a video of Sue telling her story at
master.mysevenstories.com/courses/sevenstories

The acid test for personal stories

How do we know if our personal story is having a positive effect? The acid test is the story you get in response from your future customer. You must pass the storytelling opportunity over to them. 'What about you? How did you get into this game?' If they in turn open up to share personal information in their story, then you have made a powerful connection. Give yourself a pat on the back. In Sue's case the response was a resounding 'Welcome to my world! Let's go find a whiteboard ...'

Be aware that if you tell a two-minute personal story, the responding story is likely to be longer—sometimes a lot longer. Resist the temptation to cut them short. Recognise that they haven't had the benefit of thinking about and refining their story as you have. You'll need to be patient with their raw-story response.

This begs the question, how big can a group be before it takes too long to exchange stories? You'll need to make a judgement call. It depends on group size and the expected meeting duration. In a one-on-one meeting scheduled for thirty minutes, I'm happy to tell a two-minute story and prompt for a five-minute client story. I know the rapport built in those seven minutes will be time well spent. I also know that if I share stories a thirty-minute meeting is likely to stretch to a fruitful 60 or 90 minutes, or an invitation for a follow-up meeting. If there are two representatives from each company and my people have practised their stories, then a four-way story exchange could take about 15 minutes. I'd be happy with that time expenditure in a 60-minute meeting. At a certain group size or time limit, I might choose to tell my story but not prompt for responding stories. Later, if there is an opportunity to catch people one-on-one, I'll refer to a part of my story and ask for theirs. 'What about you—how did you get started in this business?'

There are a couple of ways a story exchange can go wrong.

Death by story

Early in my consulting career, I was fired up about story-telling and decided to do a story exchange with a group of ten people. I'd introduced one of my IT company clients to one of my past customers, a mining company executive. I facilitated a one-day workshop to help the IT company learn from the mining executive because they wanted to test a business strategy on a 'captive' client. The back-story of the mining exec was interesting and relevant to the workshop—the backstory of the eight IT company employees, less so.

As we went around the group, listening to a hodge-podge of stories, I realised I'd made a mistake. There was no future benefit from sharing everyone's story, because there was little chance of a future business relationship. We were wasting time, but I was stuck. Once you start a round of storytelling it's difficult to cut it short, as everyone expects a chance to tell their story.

Another way group story sharing can go wrong is when one of the group members 'overshares'.

An oversharing story

Some years ago I was in a one-day team strategy meeting with about thirty executives from our company. Our managing director had hired a facilitator for the workshop and the first session was a 'getting to know you' exercise. Each of us in turn had to list the high and low points of our career, plot them on a graph and present the graph to the group.

One of my colleagues decided to share details of his divorce, the death of his second wife from cancer and various other calamities. He broke down in tears in front of the group. That was uncomfortable for everyone.

The group was too large for that story. You might choose to include deeply personal story events in a one-on-one meeting, but as group size increases it becomes more difficult and I recommend a more business-oriented story.

When to avoid personal stories

Personal story sharing works best in small groups, face to face. They can be effective in a telephone call but not when cold calling. If you interrupt someone who isn't expecting your call, the last thing they want to hear is your personal story! The perfect cold calling story is either an insight story or a success story. You'll learn about those story types in the next part, but cold calling is not within the scope of this book. Mike Bosworth's 'peer story' for the materials manager, which you read in the foreword, is an example of a cold-calling success story. (We teach prospecting in our Story Prospecting online course.[3])

Personal stories work brilliantly in presentations to large groups, but you'll need to leave the story sharing to more intimate encounters.

Public story workshops

I'd like to explain how we run our public story workshops because it will give you insight into how to create your own personal and key staff stories. In our one-day public workshops we devote more than half of the time for each student to construct their personal story, because it teaches them the critical skills of story sharing and interviewing. Our group of about twelve people split into pairs and students take turns to interview each other to uncover the other's personal story, seeking out the good stuff. The interviewer will then present the other person's story to the group. Each interview runs for between twenty and twenty-five minutes, then they swap roles. When we get the group back together we listen to each personal story as told by the interviewer.

Everyone in the group has a chance to comment on every story. I ask them to focus on three aspects while they are listening:

1. **The story.** How did it grab them? Was it interesting? Did it follow the story structure?

2. **The story's subject.** What else would you like to know about them? What do you think about them now?

3. **The delivery.** How was it presented? What does the presentation say about the presenter?

When I go around the room the first person I ask is the subject of the story. 'How did it feel to have your story told by someone else? Would you tell it that way?' It's an invaluable experience to hear someone else tell your story and to have a dozen people comment on it in an open discussion. And it is a lot more useful than trying to create your story on your own.

Some people are good at telling their stories, but many are uncomfortable hearing their story told and need help. When we've heard and commented on every story I ask the group to reflect on the overall experience. How did it feel to hear those stories? How do you feel now about your student cohort? If you heard such a story from a potential customer, what would that be like?

Every time there is one overwhelming sentiment from the group; 'Wow! Every single story is interesting!' In three years of story workshops we've never had an uninteresting story. Every one of them is interesting, and everyone is interested. They all lean in, listening with intent. They're not distracted. It makes a mockery of the fear of wasting a few minutes on telling your story. Here is a group of twelve business people, often people who work together, whom you might expect to know each other, listening intently and responding with a wide range of emotions. That tells you something. Personal stories are fascinating. We think our own story isn't interesting, but we're wrong.

In these group sessions the interviewer has twenty-five minutes to interview and ten minutes to prepare, and they usually deliver a three- to six-minute story, which is mostly too long for a business setting. There's still work to do to refine the story, but it's an excellent start. If you don't have the benefit of a story workshop, you can still incorporate some of these ideas by working with a friend or colleague and then sharing with a wider group. I've found that public groups of strangers interact better than groups of work colleagues. It's harder to be vulnerable in front of your work colleagues.

Record, refine, reflect

As you refine your personal story I recommend writing it out to help you tighten it. Then video yourself telling the story so you can hear how it sounds. We use video messaging apps like WhatsApp to do this. When you record yourself telling the story you'll see how long it really takes, because we're hopeless at judging duration.

Your target should be somewhere between two and three minutes. You may need to force yourself to listen to the video, as it can be uncomfortable, but there are important questions to ask yourself:

- What overall point does my story make about me?

- Is it an authentic story about who I am?

- Does the story explain why I do what I do?

- Am I too much of a hero in my story?

- Do I display human weaknesses and vulnerabilities?

- What is really personal in my story?

- Does the story demonstrate what I could do for a future client?

- Am I positioned as an authority or a conduit to useful resources?

There is another benefit to videoing your story. Repeated listening, deleting, revising and even starting again is essential for you to properly internalise the story. Only then will you be comfortable and confident in delivering it. Finally, share your story drafts with friends to get multiple opinions. Most people need that level of comfortable familiarity before they deliver their personal story for the first time in an important business meeting.

By now you may have some questions. Like, is it really worth putting this much effort into my personal story? And isn't the whole process manipulative? Yes, it is worth the effort, because it will become the foundation of every effective business connection you make. And yes, in a sense it is manipulative. We're presenting a view of ourselves that we've spent time thinking about and crafting. We're not telling the full story, because that's not possible, and we're not dwelling on things that would undermine our authority.

The interesting thing, though, is that these stories are like lie detectors. When we tell a story about something that happened to us, we relive those moments in our mind. We recall the emotion of the event, and that emotion comes out in our voice. If we're telling a true story, the voice tone is authentic and the story sounds credible. If we're not being authentic, that too is detectable.

We select moments that actually happened in our lives and deliver them authentically as a way to connect. We tell the truth and respect our listener because we are communicating in the brain's natural language, in a sequence, in a way that is easy to assimilate. The listener re-creates and co-experiences the events with us.

Being selective is essential. You can have multiple (true) personal stories you can draw on in different circumstances. You might identify five or ten events that have been pivotal to your career. The question is which events to choose to put into your story. That's where having a friend act as a sounding board really helps. They respect you, know the sort of person you are and have your best interests at heart. They'll help you choose the right topics, though this will also depend on the meeting circumstances, as some parts of your story will resonate more with some people than with others. I adjust my personal story depending on the industry of the person I'm connecting with. It makes sense to select events from my past that my new client can relate to.

In the personal story we're trying to find a balance between revealing who we are and indicating how we can assist the listener, all without explicitly referencing these aims. If we do this effectively, the payback is a type of friendship and support through the buying process from a new friend. Are you the sort of person who takes advantage of your friends? I'm sure you are not—we look after our friends. The story exchange doesn't just make you likeable and credible in the eyes of your client; it also connects the client to you. They become someone you care about. When you've shared stories you'll be looking for outcomes that benefit you both.

PERSONAL STORY INTERVIEW— STEPS AND QUESTIONS
Tell me about your childhood?
What did you want to be when you grew up?
What did you study? Why?
What was your first job?
What was your first relevant job?
Tell me about it?
Tell me about you most memorable successes? How did you feel?
What about failures and setbacks? How did you feel?
Do you know what you really want to do now? Why?
What annoys you?
What inspires you?
What will be your legacy?
Where will you be in five years' time?
Is there anything you'd like to share about your personal life?
If you could be an animal, which would you choose?

Figure 6.1: Personal story interview cheat sheet

Key staff stories: bragging allowed!

Key staff are trusted individuals in your company who are critical to the business opportunity. Very often they will be technical experts, though in a smaller company it may devolve to the CEO. In large technology companies the 'Cisco approach' is commonly used, with the selling done in pairs. A salesperson is paired with a technical sales expert for client meetings. The personal story of that technical expert, told either by themselves or by the salesperson, is important for the client's technical team. I explained in chapter 4 that key staff stories *prime* your future client to accept the authority of important actors in the sales and post-sales phase.

To uncover your key staff stories, you will use the same interview process you learned while developing your personal story. Why are key staff stories important? Well, assuming your future client knows you are the salesperson, you will (unhappily) have the least credibility. Those with the most credibility for your client are the technical people who really understand your solution and the operations people who will deliver it. Your future client needs to know about these people as early as possible in the process.

Who should deliver the key staff story?

The international expert

For our first public story workshop I invited friends and past colleagues to come along. One participant was Alan, the brother of a family friend. When I called Alan about the workshop he was enthusiastic: 'I truly believe in storytelling. I use it all the time!'

Alan told me about his role as the only Australian representative for an overseas software company. 'I had used the software myself in a previous company and loved it. So when I met potential clients I just told them the story of my experience; needing a solution, surveying the market and falling in love with that product.'

Alan had no trouble creating interest, but he wasn't able to run a trial or answer detailed technical questions, so an expert was brought in from overseas. As they worked together, Alan could see that this technical specialist was not connecting with his client's technical people. His lack of English language fluency was making a bad impression.

That was frustrating because Alan knew his technical guy had tremendous, relevant experience. Alan coached his technical specialist to tell his personal story about how he became expert in that technology.

After the coaching they both told their personal stories and the clients shared their stories. Alan and his colleague had huge success opening up the market in Australia.

You appreciate from this story that best person to deliver the key staff story is that key person! But they are unlikely to deliver a good story without coaching and practice, and sometimes they are not available to tell their story in person, in which case you must tell it.

There are a few important differences between telling your own career story and telling someone else's. Your own story can be more personal because you own it. Your key staff stories will focus more on their business career, not least because you must respect their privacy. On the other hand, you need not flinch from bragging in a key staff story, so pump them up! Select the parts of their story that show them in the best light.

> **Don't flinch from bragging about your key staff in their story, pump them up!**

For those who struggle to tell their personal story in under three minutes, I recommend breaking it into two or three parts, and delivering the parts in a story exchange. It is easier to abridge key staff stories to one or two minutes and deliver them in one go.

Company creation story — ask the right questions

How do we set about devising a company creation story? Of course the answer depends on the history, size and leadership of your company. Easiest, in terms of story research, is if the company was founded by one or two people who are still active in the company and available to be interviewed. It gets more complicated as your company grows and cycles through leaders. If you work for a large, well-known corporation like Apple or Google, the founders and founding story will be familiar to all, but you can always focus on a more specific story such as the development of your technology area within the corporation or the company's story in a specific geographical region, like my story of Schlumberger in Russia. Every company has interesting stories; it's just a matter of asking the right questions.

COMPANY CREATION STORY— STEPS AND QUESTIONS
Record all interviews.
Identify the key players.
Do you have access to the founders?
Who is the company storyteller? Interview that person.
Access public company records for key dates.
Why was the company founded?
Where and when was it founded?
What were the business and personal objectives?
What had the founders done previously?
What were their guiding principles?
What was special about their background?
What were the early days like?
Were there any failures? (Get the full story.)
Why did the company succeed?
Describe a key early success. (Get the full story.)
Was there a turning point?
Who were their early customers? (Can you interview them?)
What are its key statistics?
Where is the company now?
Where is the company going?

Figure 6.2: Company creation story cheat sheet

I'm going to take you through three different company stories to give you a sense of these stories, and you can adapt your company story approach from one or more of these examples.

The founder's story

You will remember Sue telling her personal story to Matt, the owner of an international oil and gas technology company, earlier in this chapter. Matt's company became a client, and one of our first projects was to write their company story. For this purpose, we conducted a two-hour interview with Matt and three or four of his executive team. Matt regaled us with story after story about the near failures and calamities of his now successful business. True to type, Matt is an excellent storyteller.

His company history is a variation of the Silicon Valley 'born in a garage' story made famous by the likes of HP, Apple and Microsoft. In Australia it starts in a shed.

Inspiration downunder

In the early 2000s, Matt was working as a geophysicist at BHP Petroleum. He was also adjunct associate professor of geophysics at Curtin University in Perth. Keen to start his own geophysics software business, Matt saw in PhD student Troy a potential partner with a brilliant mind who could 'do anything'. Matt and Troy were working on software techniques to 'invert' seismic acoustic survey data to a quantitatively useful parameter such as the probability of hydrocarbon. In late 2003, Matt left BHP and together with Troy, founded Downunder GeoSolutions (DUG).

Processing seismic data requires banks of computers to perform parallel computations on terabytes of data. Matt and Troy installed a network of PC computers in a shed they built in Matt's backyard. They immediately encountered an overheating problem with their massed PC computers. The solution was to stack the PCs on their sides, fit the shed roof with an array of exhaust fans sourced from the local hardware store, and drape a curtain from the window to direct outside air up through the PCs to cool them. After about three months, the processor boards started turning green from the humid air and within a year they fell apart, but the first DUG supercomputer had done its job.

The company struggled to make money in the early years, surviving on grants and piecemeal consulting projects. Then in 2006, Matt and Troy had an opportunity to apply their technique to a data set from Western Australia for US oil and gas giant Apache. Three dry holes had been drilled in the licence area and Apache had an obligation to drill one more well before they could relinquish the licence.

Matt and Troy took on the job with more bravado than confidence, and after six months of processing they produced the world's first hydrocarbon probability volume map. Their interpretation showed why the initial wells had failed, and Apache used their results to drill the first discovery well and a further 18 accurately predicted oil and gas wells. The Julimar oil and gas field, which now supplies gas to the $30 billion Wheatstone liquid natural gas plant, is the result. This success launched the company, allowing Matt and Troy to open new global offices and invest in new supercomputers, expand their processing capability and take on new customers.

Today the company has outgrown the shed! DUG has grown to 350 employees and is the third largest seismic processing company in the world, and the largest land seismic processing company in the United States. They operate a network of massive supercomputers in London,

Houston, Kuala Lumpur and Perth, each cooled with DUG-patented oil cooling baths, and service the seismic processing needs of oil and gas companies around the world.

Notice that this story follows the simple story framework.

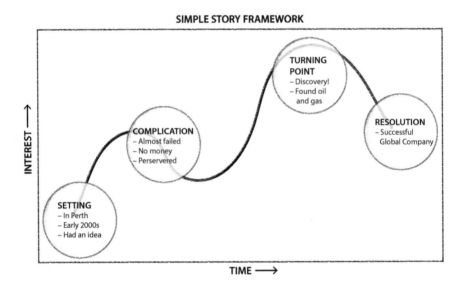

Figure 6.3: The DUG company creation story

Matt and Troy are the heroes of the story and they're still active in the company. Let's review some of the messages delivered within this story:

- The company has an interesting history.

- The company could easily have failed and had some good fortune (which is true of every successful company).

- The founders are innovative and smart. By implication, the company itself is innovative and smart.

- It's a software and a hardware company, both of which are developed in-house.

- They operate supercomputers throughout the world.

- The company has grown to a scale where it can support any type of oil and gas client anywhere in the world.

Of course, a DUG salesperson could assert each of these things, but a story will always be more engaging and memorable. In a story, each of these messages will be assimilated by a listener without the pushback that would be likely if a salesperson was doing the 'telling'.

Let's look at a situation in which you do not want to focus on the founder's exploits because the founder is no longer in the company or is playing only a minor role.

The established company story

Our first consulting client was (and still is) a property services company called First5minutes. They specialise in fire and emergency compliance for commercial buildings. The founder of the company was with the company for only a couple of years, and when I started researching it the company story wasn't known by any of the sales team. To uncover the story, I tracked down past employees and put together a timeline using publicly available company records. Here's the long form.

Five minutes to disaster

On Sunday, 21 April 1985, fireman Ralf was in his Queensland Sunshine Coast home watching TV when a news item came on about a fire at the Hamilton Island resort. As Ralf watched chaotic scenes of panicked tourists, he had an idea for a business.

Ralf knew that new regulations required commercial property owners to properly inform occupants about the escape routes and use of emergency equipment, so he put together a fire warden training program and signed up several customers. But he struggled with the business aspects of the venture and he soon ran out of money. A major shareholder was brought in to manage the business.

The new owners wanted to divest the fire compliance company and Tony, with his business partner David, purchased the business and set about investing the capital needed to develop the services and build an expert team to deliver them, backed up by quality management systems. The company was renamed First5Minutes, inspired by a fire training video about the 1985 Bradford City soccer stadium fire in the UK.[4] From an initial cigarette spark, the main stand, seating thousands of fans, burned to the ground in less than five minutes. Fifty-six fans died. That tragedy could have been avoided if fire extinguishers and hoses had been available to people who knew how to use them and if the fans had been properly directed to escape exits.

The late 1980s was the perfect time to start a building compliance business. There was a boom in high-rise office and apartment buildings, and new fire regulations required all building owners to install approved safety systems. Early customers, such as AMP and National Australia Bank, also had compliance needs in Sydney and Melbourne, and for a while trainers were flown in from Brisbane, until local offices were set up. First5minutes is now the preeminent company in its field, operating from its own offices in each of the mainland Australian capital cities.

In 2014, when a gunman took hostages at a Martin Place café in Sydney, the police needed urgent access to the plans of the building where the hostages were held. In the building entranceway was a First5minutes evacuation map with emergency contact details. The police contacted the building owner and First5minutes provided instant access to online building plans. Those plans were critical to resolving the crisis.

Every salesperson in First5minutes is asked to learn this story when they join the company. They tell the story in their own words, but we ensure they practise with video messages until they are fluent.

What messages are contained in the story?

- Emergency response within the first five minutes is critical.

- Protection is a key company value.

- First5minutes has grown with the fire compliance regulations in Australia.

- The company is committed to building safety.

- The company has large, well-known clients.

- It has modern online systems.

- It's the largest and leading company in its sector.

- You can trust First5minutes.

The big corporation story

The largest corporations have books written about them, so there is no problem with research. The issue is what to include in the story. It's a selection problem. I recommend including the basics of the company's creation story but then telling the technology, geography or service story that is most relevant to your sales opportunity.

Schlumberger is the largest service company in the oil and gas industry. In 2016 it had a staff of 100,000 and generated nearly

$30 billion in revenue. Everyone in the oil and gas industry has heard of Schlumberger, although that doesn't mean everyone knows the company story or has a clear understanding of what they do, or even likes them. It's your responsibility to properly introduce your company. If you refer back to my story about Schlumberger in Russia in chapter 4, you'll notice that the first paragraph is about how the company was founded. The subsequent paragraphs focus on the history of Schlumberger in Russia, which was my sales territory.

What messages are contained in the Schlumberger Russia story?

- Schlumberger is a well-established company in the industry.

- Theirs is one of the most famous stories in the oil and gas industry.

- The company has overcome adversity and will continue to do so.

- It invests in its markets.

- The business outcomes for its customers have been outstanding—they'll make you rich!

- Wouldn't you (my customer) like to be part of this success?

The company story exchange

Just as with personal stories, the company story is an opportunity to exchange stories. The history of your client's company or division is useful to know. 'Enough about us—what about your company? How did you get started?' If you get that history in a story you're likely to remember it, and that's more useful than you might at first realise.

For a start, their company story often includes important clues about the values and culture of the organisation you want to do business with. And there are other benefits. In the next part you'll learn about success stories, and knowing your client's company story helps you construct and tell success stories. Furthermore, my clients often ask me about other clients I work with. When they do, I tell my client's company story. They enjoy hearing it and several times I've been able to make business connections between my clients.

You must tell your story!

It should go without saying that all efforts to research and create a story are wasted if you don't tell the story but I often encounter that situation. I work with salespeople to prepare their stories, then at that important first meeting they fail to tell the story. They're frightened, afraid of wasting time, of revealing too much about themselves, of an adverse response. They worry about the content and about the ideal delivery time. It all adds up to a fear of rejection and fear of the unknown by moving outside their comfort zone.

I see similar fears and get similar objections from salespeople who have to phone someone they don't know. You must overcome these fears or you can't be a salesperson. It's that simple. Your story-telling (and telephoning) get better with practice. You'll be amazed and surprised at how effective your stories are. But only if you tell them!

Hook story checklist

✓ Have you lived? Good! Tell your story.

✓ Are there other people in your company who your future client needs to trust? Tell their stories.

✓ Do you work for a company or organisation? Tell that story.

✓ Then share! 'Enough about me … what about you?'

✓ Upload your company and key staff stories to your story library so everyone in the team can access the stories.

Part 3

FIGHT
Winning Mindshare

In this part:

Insight stories

Success stories

7. Why you? Why your company?

Insight is an unexpected shift to a better story.

Gary Klein, Author and Research Psychologist

In the previous part of this book, we talked about making a personal and company connection with your future client. That's critical, because then they'll listen to you. Now you need to position your products and services so you are offering the *only* solution to the buyer's problems.

To do that means changing your future customer's mind in two ways. First, you need them to appreciate and understand the insights you have about their business and what is special about what your company can do for them. That's problematic because your future client thinks they already know their business, so why would they accept that you have any useful insights? But every vendor has special insights about its customers; if it didn't, it wouldn't survive long as a business. You use insight stories for this mind change. Second, you need them to picture what it will feel like when they use your products and services. What will a solution be like for them? To understand that, they need to experience your solution in their mind ahead of time. That's where success stories come in, and they also changes minds.

These, then, are the two types of stories we're going to learn about in this part. An insight story explains a perspective you have of their business that they don't quite appreciate. Your insights are 'commercial' grade if your company is uniquely positioned to take business advantage of them. *Commercial insight* is knowledge about an aspect of your customer's business that they should know about and that your company can uniquely address.[1] The success story is a story you tell of someone else receiving the benefits of your products and services, and what it meant for their life and their business. Success stories allow your client to mentally project into the future, experience your solution and convince themselves that it's safe and profitable to pursue that outcome.

> **Success stories allow your client to mentally project into the future and convince themselves that it's safe and profitable to pursue that outcome.**

Every sales manager and salesperson has a pipeline of possible future business, but a significant proportion of that business never happens. That has been a fact of life in every sales team I've ever worked in or for. The common reason most pipeline deals don't close is that in the mind of the salesperson, the deal is done. They are confident this client would benefit from buying their products and services, but they have yet to convert the buyer to this conviction. The vendor organisation can see the client's case for change, but the client cannot see it. The challenge is to create a change in the mind of the buyer, and that's what this part of the book is about. I call it the Fight stage of the deal.

It is a fight because you must fight for the client's mindshare, and you will have competition! Buyers are busy; their minds are deeply engaged in their business. They're of the view that they know what they're doing. They usually *do* know what they're doing.

So why should they change? What is it that you bring to them that may convince them to change? The only reason they would change is if they get an idea, an insight, about how something could be different and then *persuade themselves* that it's worth taking the risk to make that change.

Buying is a merger of world views

Your buyer will not change unless convinced there is a clear reason to do so. Without this clear reason you're not going to sell them anything. That's fundamental. Your buyers have their own ideas about the world, how it works and the constraints they face, and their world view doesn't match your view of how the world could be for them.

In our consultancy, we are often asked to help our clients assess and select new salespeople. To assess the skills of a sales recruit we put them through a realistic sales simulation. One of the insights we have is that most sales managers and business owners don't appreciate that they're not good at assessing the skills of sales candidates. Our insight is that observing a salesperson perform in a realistic selling situation and analysing their performance against a benchmark is the best test. Of course, merely asserting that sales leaders are incompetent would not get us far. We need an insight story.

Hiring salespeople

Around the time we started our business, in 2014, I met Paul, the owner of a telecommunications software company, at an industry awards event. Paul was in the process of hiring a head of sales. His business was rapidly expanding internationally and he needed a sales manager to build an international team. I showed Paul our method for evaluating sales conversation skill and he engaged us to evaluate six candidates by video conference. Two of them demonstrated excellent skills and Paul hired both—one as head of sales and one as head of marketing.

Ten months later, Steve, one of those excellent, well-trained conversationalists, asked me to do a similar evaluation for two sales candidates he was considering. Neither tested well. When Steve watched the video of each candidate attempting to sell he was shocked! In his words, it was 'sobering to watch'. Even though Steve himself had tested well, he didn't have the skill to assess sales competence just from an interview.

The insight in this example is that you must assess sales conversation skills by means of a structured test. We can call this a commercial insight because our consulting company has a methodology and a service that addresses that insight. Steve himself had the required conversation skills, but he was unable to evaluate a candidate via a standard interview process. In response to this insight, Steve routinely evaluates sales candidates using a simulation test, and his international sales team is going from strength to strength.

If I need to explain to a potential client about the importance of conversation skills testing, I simply tell that story. I don't make claims. I don't assert that 'interviews are an ineffective way to assess sales skills' or 'interviews are only 31 percent effective in uncovering critical sales skills'. These facts are unlikely to be accepted, because most hiring managers think they're good at selecting salespeople. It's the way our minds work. We forget all the bad hires and only remember the ones that worked out well. We have an idea of our performance that is better than it actually is. It wasn't until Steve watched candidates fail at the simulation that he got the insight. Others don't need to undergo the same experience as Steve—they can learn from his experience through the insight story. When they hear it as a story, they're not threatened. They relax into the story and are receptive to the insight. Without the story, they don't get it.

Changing beliefs

We talked earlier about the common view that a coherent set of facts are persuasive in themselves. Buyers could go to our website, read the facts and be persuaded by them, but that's not how people change their minds. They need a narrative to expand their way of thinking. By definition, your insight is new and surprising. The narrative must take them from where their current thinking lies on a journey to appreciating the insight.

> **An insight story takes your client from their current thinking on a journey to appreciating the insight.**

But what if we need to change a strongly held belief? If your insight contradicts your client's firm belief, you have a most difficult challenge.

When we believe something strongly, we protect ourselves against new facts that conflict with our model. We can twist just about anything to suit our beliefs. So how do we help someone with a strong belief to see things from a different perspective?

Several studies have looked at how we defend our beliefs from contradictory evidence. One study examined a group of partisan Republican and Democrat supporters at the time of the 2004 US presidential election.[2] Researchers observed their study participants brains with a functional magnetic resonance imaging machine (fMRI) while they were read contradictory statements about candidates from each side of the political divide. The research subjects easily identified contradictions in their non-preferred candidates, but failed to recognise them in their preferred candidates.

A more recent fMRI study by a team that included neuroscientist and public intellectual Sam Harris, found that test subjects were far more resistant to counterarguments on political, religious and moral topics than on non-political beliefs. The study found that defending one's beliefs against challenging evidence is a form of internally directed cognition involving both disconnection from externally presented evidence and a search through memory for relevant counterarguments.[3]

What if stories are used as counterarguments rather than counter-facts? Even that has been studied using an MRI scanner!

Belief brainwaves

In 2017, a team headed by Jonas Kaplan published an article called 'Processing Narratives Concerning Protected Values'.[4] The team wanted to understand how narratives influence 'protected values', such as values related to core personal, national and religious beliefs.

They recruited 78 American, Iranian and Chinese test subjects, who were read real-life stories while in an MRI machine (the Iranian and Chinese cohorts were recent immigrants to the Unites States). When the participants felt that the hero of the story was encountering a (self-reported) protected value, specific areas of the cortex known to be involved in social and moral thinking were more active compared with normal story plot twists and the participants took longer to answer. This effect was seen in each ethnic group, although the effect strength varied by group.

These studies show that new facts and one-off storytelling won't change committed beliefs. A set of beliefs constitutes a consistent model in the mind of the believer built up over their lifetime by personal experience, popular stories, myths, fables and parables. And there can be hidden motives for holding those beliefs[5]—showing loyalty to their group, for example. Assertions that don't fit the model will bounce off. To have any chance of changing firm beliefs, you must provide new experiences and new stories.

I suspect that story *sharing* is essential to bridging the gap between parties who hold widely differing beliefs. Maybe there'll be a story sharing experiment in the scanner next?

Insight selling

In the past few years insight selling has gained a higher profile in the sales world, promoted by sales consulting companies such as RAIN Group[6], with their book *Insight Selling*[7], and the Corporate Executive Board (CEB)[8] through *The Challenger Sale* and *The Challenger Customer*. The *Challenger* books focus on challenging your buyer's beliefs by offering them insights into their business that haven't occurred to them. *Challenger Customer* does an excellent job of explaining how to develop commercial insight, and I recommend it for business developers. *Challenger Customer* is less convincing on how to deliver that insight to a potential client. The sample 'conversations' don't ring true to me. If you think about it, it's a sensitive exercise: you have to present yourself as more knowledgeable than your client concerning an aspect of their business.

The trick is to tell the story of how you uncovered your insights, including all the trials and errors and false starts. It should also outline the history of how you persuaded other clients of the validity of your insights. When you take your buyer on this journey, they don't push back. They appreciate and assimilate the insights.

The best insight stories deliver the experience of finding the insight and these stories are the mark of the best salespeople.

Then a success story

Success stories are the other key element of the Fight phase. These stories change your buyer's mind by allowing them to experience the benefits of your products and services vicariously, without any cost to themselves. They learn how someone in a similar situation to them followed your guidance, and succeeded. They are, in fact, changing their minds, rewiring their cortex as they assimilate the story and understand how your solution could work for them.

This is very important, because without this story it's unlikely your buyer will take the risk of purchasing your products or services. They are thinking, 'Why would I take this step? What might go wrong? Maybe it's the wrong thing to do.' The story lets them picture the possible rewards, and that reduces their anxiety about change.

In the two-step process that is the Fight phase, first tell an insight story to show a possible new way of conducting business, then a success story to persuade the buyer that it's safe to proceed, because someone like them succeeded.

Applying insight

In my experience across many industries, vendor organisations tend to think insight is inherent in their products and services. They think they have 'bottled' insight. That's not right. Insight is about your client's business and how they perform that business. To find insight, you must talk with your clients with a curious mind.

Public private insight

When I started in the facility services industry, one of my goals was to win business with one of the world's largest mining companies in a major mining area in Australia. My background was in technology companies, I didn't know much about the facility services business, but I knew enough to seek out an insightful angle. I met Andrew, the mining company manager in charge of all accommodation in my target mining area. Andrew was responsible for housing tens of thousands of people in townships and camps valued at $3 billion.

The curious thing about Andrew's business was that from an outsider's perspective it was cyclically dysfunctional. When the commodity price was high, Andrew's company spent like crazy on accommodation assets but it was difficult to get labour and prices skyrocketed. Our company, for example, had been contracted to refurbish houses at a price that was double the cost of a new house. Conversely, when the commodity price was low, the mining company stopped all spending and the houses fell into disrepair. This dysfunctional management cycle had been going on for decades. Andrew was fully aware of the problem, but he didn't know what to do about it.

Initially I just thought, *well, that's an interesting fact of life in the mining business*, but almost unconsciously my mind started working on the problem. I can't explain how this mental process happens. Back in Melbourne at our company headquarters, I was getting to know some of the other departments outside the resources sector. I encountered a business structure called a Public Private Partnership, or PPP.[9] Governments use PPPs to get large infrastructure projects, such as hospitals, prisons, bridges and highways designed, constructed and operational. A PPP is a deal structure that involves both government and private financing and includes long-term operation and maintenance of the completed infrastructure, often for twenty years or more.

PPP deals are typically awarded to a consortium consisting of a construction company, a financing company and a services company to maintain and operate the facility. My company was highly experienced on the operations side, having won about thirty social infrastructure projects such as hospitals and prisons. We had a very good business in PPPs. I wanted to understand why and how PPPs worked, because the legal and partnership structure is complex and expensive to set up.

A major reason PPPs work so well is that governments have a cyclical investment problem. Parliamentary governments are subject to election cycles, which means they can change every three to four years. As a result, they're often unable to implement long-term infrastructure projects because their political opponents will often (on principle) oppose and/or cancel a project once they get into power. At great cost to the community. The twenty-year PPP contract structure breaks that cycle and has performed brilliantly for governments.

My insight was to notice that the contracting methodology employed by governments with PPPs might also work in the resources industry, with the mining company playing the role of 'public', or government, in the public–private partnership. The mining company would contract with a consortium to deliver, maintain, and operate new and existing accommodation assets over a twenty-year period, which would smooth out the investment cycle.

That was the concept we took to Andrew and his team. The story I told was of a successful hospital project. That insight was eventually incorporated in a deal valued around three billion dollars. Unfortunately the business went to a different supplier, as my company was taken over before the deal could be landed. But that's another story.

This example illustrates how insight is focused on the customer's situation and is a problem-solving exercise that involves looking for analogous situations. The beautiful thing about insights is that when you have them you stand in a unique position with your client, because no one else has that understanding. And whoever comes up with the insight is assumed to be the one who can implement it. You get a lot of leeway to demonstrate you can solve your client's issue. In this case, we had fantastic access to Andrew and his management team.

Delivering insight

We invited the mining company management to Melbourne and workshopped the PPP concept with them. Our primary communication tool was a story about a particular hospital and how the government had figured out that the PPP structure was the right way to go. We equated the government's situation with the mining company's and let the mining company executives experience the insight of PPP through the story.

How do we distinguish between an insight story and a success story, because this story also sounds like a success story? It's an insight story because it illuminated an aspect of my client's business that they hadn't appreciated. Insight often uncovers a new idea that no one has thought of, let alone actioned, so there may yet be no success story to refer to. If you tell the insight story in a way that your client buys into it, you have a chance, but the deal still may not happen. We were in a difficult sales situation. Even though governments had succeeded with the PPP structure, no mining company had ever tackled that kind of contract. We had a fight on our hands.

Why fight with stories? Suppose your client accepts that they should do business in a new way, but there is no unique insight in your approach? If you're not able to demonstrate unique insight—that is, insight that only your company can take advantage of—then you could face stiff competition. This may mean that only price differentiates you from your competitors, which puts your profit at risk. Differentiating with unique insight is a way to capture margin. Insight is what delivers profit to your business. Maybe you have no great insight but you are able to persuade your buyer that their success will come with lower risk from your solution. Lower risk also provides a way to preserve margin, so both insight and success stories can lead to more profit.

Keep in mind that the default decision in any organisation is to do nothing, and the larger the organisation, the more likely this will be their decision. If there is no compelling insight and no clear path to success, there will be no action from your buyer.

What do people typically do in the Fight stage? Many salespeople think, *My business is generic, our competitors are the same as us. I need a discount!* I say, you might be surprised! Insights are not about new features or technology. They're often simple ideas around new ways of doing business. People intuitively understand that insight gives them a magic card, and they want that, but they're often not prepared to do the work to find that magic card.

Success stories vs case studies

Success stories are commonly confused with case studies, but they are quite different. A success story is a narrative told from the perspective of a client who achieved the success. Case studies have become formulaic marketing tools. 'This was the situation, this is what we did, and here's how great things are now. (Aren't we wonderful.)' Situation, solution, result. Them, us, us.

I had a client who displayed nicely framed case studies down two walls of the company's reception area—maybe a hundred of them. My client called them success stories, but they were couched as vendor successes. There was compelling social proof in the sheer number of client logos, but these case studies would not engage a prospective client, because they were all written from the perspective of the vendor.

Important client details were missing. Individuals in the client organisation were not named, nor was their emotional journey described. There was no sequence of events, no narrative. Important questions were not asked or answered. Why couldn't the client solve their problem on their own? How did they struggle with the issue? How did they feel about the change? How do they feel now? We don't know, because case studies throw away the good stuff.

A success narrative is not like that. A narrative of success starts with a character (your client hero) who has a problem. We learn about the hero's problem and what is at stake. A guide (your company) comes along and gives the hero a plan to lead them past potential failure to success. That's quite different from a case study. The important distinction is that the client is the hero of the story, not the vendor. It's difficult for people who supply products and services to allow their client to be the hero of their story, but it's critical they do so.

The other key is that the case study format—situation, what we did, results—is not a narrative. It's like bullet points. Bullet points are assertions, not narrative, because there is no sequence of events. A story has drama, pain, problems to overcome. The journey is what your prospective customer wants to read about. Turn your case studies into success stories and they will be fascinating for your future client. You won't need hundreds of them—just one will be persuasive.

> **Turn your case studies into success stories and they will be fascinating for your future client.**

The process of finding commercial insight is well described in *Challenger Customer*. The book explains how to map your clients' business process, understand them, look at the data from different angles and see if, given the knowledge of your products and services, you could do things a better way. Let's look at one of the examples from the book. I'll paraphrase the background.

The example is about a firm that manufactures and supplies surgical equipment for dentists and developed a new, lightweight, cable-free, battery-operated dental tool. Dentists loved the new technology but didn't see a need to change. So the firm decided to take a detailed look at the benefits of the new tool by surveying users. They discovered that dental nurses preferred to use the lightweight tool because many were experiencing injuries using the old, heavier equipment. By examining the dental nurse injury rates, they were able to quantify the benefits of the lightweight equipment in terms of injury prevention, higher job satisfaction and lower absenteeism for dental nurses.

Dentists normally would not have given much thought to nurse absenteeism related to dental equipment. The firm had a real insight to take to their market.

So what does the book recommend? They suggest their salespeople engage the dentists in a question-and-answer style of conversation. The salesperson is trained with a script that goes something like this: 'I want to talk today about some new findings we've had in our research into the true cost of hygienist absentees. We're finding that virtually all the dentists we've worked with have had the same issue, and I'm guessing you're seeing it too?'[10] (A manipulative question.) 'Well, let me show you what's actually kind of scary ...' Then they show the data. The dentist is supposed to say, 'Holy mackerel, I never knew it!' and purchase on the spot.

To me, that's simply unrealistic. A conversation in which I reveal data that shows you don't know your business is by definition problematic. The dentist is unlikely to react well to this script. If, however, the salesperson were to tell the story about how the insight was discovered, it would not be threatening. How exactly was that insight discovered? Who found it? Who did the research? Why were they thinking that way? What false leads were chased down? What mishaps occurred along the way? Tell that story as it happened.

'We have this guy, Fred, in our research department in Pennsylvania, who was asked to interview 700 dental nurses about their experience using different types of equipment, including both cable-connected and cable-free equipment. Fred thought the entire survey would be a waste of time but he was intrigued to see how often injuries were mentioned in the survey results. Fred redesigned the survey to get a better understanding of injury rates and was amazed to discover ...'

I'm inventing a not very exciting narrative here, but you get the idea. The story of the insight discovery lets the dentists discover the insight for themselves. You might think that the question-and-answer format proposed in *Challenger Customer* would also lead the dentist to the same conclusion, but that approach smacks of self-interest and manipulation, and risks pushback. If the salesperson tells the true story about how the insight was found, the dentist is more likely to go along for the ride, understand it and accept it.

The perfect story

How can we deliver a clever insight without sounding like a smart-arse? The answer is to make the insight discoverer the hero by describing the struggle, wrong turns and dead ends that occurred on the insight discovery journey. That also makes your hero relatable.

There are of course alternative insight story plotlines. For example, you could tell the story of another client 'discovering' your insight for themselves, as I did with Steve and the sales conversation skills evaluation story at the beginning of this chapter. Or you could tell the story of the difficulties you had in getting your insight accepted. Some of the most compelling stories in science are of this type. A fabulous example is the story about the cure for stomach ulcers.

The stomach ache story

In 1982, Barry Marshall[11], a registrar at the Royal Perth Hospital, teamed up with pathologist Robin Warren to study stomach bacteria. Together they developed a hypothesis that a particular bacterium *(H. pylori)* was the cause of stomach ulcers and gastric cancer.

At the time, it was thought that stomach ulcers were caused by stress and that bacteria could not survive in stomach acid. Marshall and Warren's hypothesis was ridiculed by the scientific and medical establishment.

After failing to cultivate the bacteria in pigs, Marshall gave himself a baseline endoscopy and drank cultured *H. pylori* extracted from an infected patient. When he developed ulcers he treated himself with a targeted antibiotic. The results and publicity from this stunt swayed the establishment and finally antibiotics were accepted as a cure for stomach ulcers. In 2005 Marshall and Warren were awarded the Nobel Prize for Medicine in recognition of their discovery.

That's an insight story! Note that the discovery alone was not enough. The compelling story is the bravery (or lunacy) of Barry Marshall in deliberately infecting himself with ulcer-causing bacteria in order to prove his case.

The struggle to get your insight accepted always makes an interesting story. If you think about it, the journey to get your insight accepted is the same journey your future client will need to take, which makes it the perfect story.

A beautiful, repeatable resource

Why is it that many salespeople don't tell insight or success stories? Why do they persist in making technical claims and assertions rather than teaching the insight with story? Why do they pitch case studies rather than success stories? I think most of them think stories are simply not business-like. They think, 'Serious business people build their case on facts.' But business people are also humans (really), and humans don't learn or understand new concepts from bullet points. Their minds aren't expanded or changed. It's not to say that facts don't work; they can, but you're relying on your future client making a significant amount of extra mental effort to put your facts together and arrive at the conclusion you hope they will. By packaging your insight and successes as stories, you deliver your solution directly to their mind. You rewire their mind and leave a lot less to chance.

The two fight stories, in tandem, represent a high level of persuasion skill. People who have the ability to tell insight and success stories in this way can take on the most difficult sales challenges. They will win the most challenging deals, manage the largest territories and be paid the most and are most likely to be promoted. Mastery of these stories is an escalator to more meaningful and consequential sales work, and to membership of an elite club.

> **Mastery of the fight stories is an escalator to more meaningful and consequential sales work, and to membership of an elite club.**

You'll change your focus from assembling facts and creating endless PowerPoint decks to finding and applying stories. With insight and success stories you don't need as many facts, which makes your job simpler! In the next two chapters I'll explain more about what these stories are and how you can create your own. There is serious work to be done, but once you have those stories, you'll have discovered a beautiful, repeatable resource that you can use again and again. You can tell them as many times as you have clients, and they'll have the same impact every time.

You may be asking, will these stories work in my situation? Of course, that depends on what sort of business yours is. Most salespeople are in a competitive business, in which their company competes with others to sell those widgets or services. If you are the only business in the field, it's usually because you are new in the market with an innovation. With no history of people buying your product, your job is harder. The insight story is critical when you are bringing a new, highly differentiated product to the market.

But let's say you're in a competitive situation and you have a lot of similar competitors. You can still find insight in your client's business. What does your client not understand about their business? Maybe your competitors could find similar insights, but are they smart enough to do so? Are they trained to deliver their insight as a story?

If you're in a competitive situation with 'me too' products and services, you need a competitive advantage. Competitive advantage can be based on the lowest price, better manufacturing or delivery capacity, the best support or the most well-known brand. All these elements are part of your competitive landscape, but you can also differentiate with your sales skills. Your ability to find insight in the client's situation and tell an insight story can make your offering unique and highly differentiated. You have the insight to show your client how to operate better. That is the path to being a trusted adviser, and it's a definite competitive advantage. It doesn't mean you always win. Maybe the competitor who offers a much lower price will win, but your chances will increase as you differentiate with fight stories.

As a salesperson you're in the business of change. Your future client will continue to do whatever they have always done, unless you can persuade them to change. Your insight stories position your company as the one that understands them best and has figured out how they must change. Your success stories lower their perception of risk and make you the safe choice. And that's going to increase your chance of winning dramatically.

**As a salesperson you're in the business of change.
Your future client will continue to do whatever they have
always done, unless you persuade them to change.**

You made a solid connection with your hook stories and now you will use fight stories to make your company the preferred supplier.

For sales leaders, winning the Fight stage is a three-step formula:

1. Arm your sales team with commercial insight.

2. Gather your successes into client-centred narratives.

3. Teach your salespeople to deliver insight and success stories.

In the next chapter we'll look in more detail at what insight and success stories are and aren't so there is no confusion.

8. Be the only option

Knowledge is a big subject. Ignorance is bigger.
And it's more interesting.

Stuart Firestein, *Ignorance: How it Drives Science*

In this chapter you'll learn what insight and success stories are and what they're not. *Insight* and *success* in the context of sales stories have specific meanings. When you know what they are, you'll know what you're looking for and have a much better chance of finding and using these powerful stories.

We have to notice, investigate and tease out these stories, but we don't just make them up. When I'm facilitating a story workshop I'm sometimes asked, 'Is it okay to make up a story?' The answer is, not if you want to maintain your credibility. It's okay to tell a fable—that is, a story that's obviously made up to make a general point—and it's quite okay to tell someone else's story. But never make up a story and pretend it's true, and don't pretend that other people's stories are your own—you will be caught out.

Some storytelling pundits will tell you that stories can be 'true' without the events themselves being true. They mean that false or altered events could still make a true business point. I agree, and that's the case with many fables, parables and myths. But *note well* who delivers those stories: they are stories told by gods, spiritual masters and famous people. Salespeople *do not rank* in the pantheon of trusted fable authorities! Our stories must be scrupulously true.

**Business stories that salespeople tell
must be scrupulously true.**

Discovering commercial insight

As we've discovered, sharing an insight story—which is essentially the story of how you discovered commercial insight about an aspect of your client's business—creates clear potential for pushback. Implying they don't know their own business won't go down so well, which is why you are using a story in the first place, so what sort of insight works best? Let's look at another example from *Challenger Customer*. Again, I'm paraphrasing.

Colourful insight

The VP of marketing for Xerox in the early 2000s was responsible for marketing a new solid ink printer called the ColorCube to the K-12 education market in North America. At first glance, Xerox's situation was a marketer's dream. They had a highly differentiated product in a market that only used black and white printers. But the VP noticed that the initial sales and marketing push based on superior technology with 'colour' was not getting traction. Education budgets around the country were tight, and the commercial managers responsible for capital purchases were not buying colour.

Research was commissioned on K-12 students (their customers' customers). They investigated the effect of colour materials on student learning outcomes. The researchers were able to show a significant link between use of colour in education materials and improved student outcomes.

The sales teams were armed with the research results and taught how to present the research to educators, rather than the traditional procurement buyers. Xerox used the response of the customer to their commercial insight (the effect of colour on learning outcomes) to determine whether or not they were talking with a 'mobiliser', someone who could mobilise their school to make a decision to purchase colour printers.

Using customer insight and the customer mobiliser approach, Xerox gained a 17 percent lift in sales in a market that had been in decline.

I've taken events described in a full chapter of *Challenger Customer* and condensed it into a narrative about the VP of marketing. There is a problem with the story, though—it's one of perspective. *Challenger Customer* was written for salespeople and the story is interesting to salespeople, but it's not an insight story. Xerox's customers are not likely to sympathise with Xerox's problem of how to sell colour copiers. Xerox's customers are interested in the research and how it relates to them. They are concerned about the business of education. How was the research conducted? Who did it? Which schools and student demographics were included in the research? How was the insight linking colour to educational outcomes discovered? That's the interesting story for Xerox's customers and it's the story the Xerox salespeople need. The facts about the research need to be embedded in the researcher's story—preferably the story of an actual researcher. Alternatively, the insight story could be about the example of a single child who used colour to overcome a learning difficulty. Educators would still need the data to back up the story, but the story of a single transformed child or classroom could be compelling.

It's important to recognise that stories about specific events are often more compelling than the weight of accumulated facts. The flood of refugees into Europe from the Syrian civil war had been escalating since 2011. But in September 2015, a photograph of a single three-year-old child[1] found dead on a Mediterranean beach galvanised European leaders to act in a more humanitarian way towards Syrian refugees.[2]

Follow the principles in *Challenger Customer* to develop your commercial insight. Then present your research findings as a discovery journey through story. Insight is a fabulous thing. It's a new way of thinking, but how the researcher arrived at that insight is the interesting and practical story to deliver.

The story behind the insight

The most famous equation in physics is Albert Einstein's $E = mc^2$. It's the simplest manifestation of one of the greatest insights in the history of science. In 1905, when Einstein was 26, physics had its *annus mirabilis* (wonderful year). Einstein published four groundbreaking papers that year. The fourth outlined in just three pages his famous equation. But what's the story behind his insight?

Einstein sees the light

Einstein was good at maths and physics at school, but he was a poor student. He failed the general entrance examination to the Swiss Federal Polytechnic and went to work as a patent clerk while he reapplied for university. He was a narrow-tracked obsessive about the things that interested him, and one of his obsessions was light. At the age of sixteen[3], he imagined what it would be like to ride on a beam of light. Surely the light wave would be frozen? Would he be surfing a frozen light wave? If he travelled at the speed of light with a mirror held in front of him, would he be invisible in the mirror? Scottish scientist James Maxwell's equations predict the speed of light as fixed at about one billion kilometres a second, so what happens as you approached that speed?

While walking with a friend in the hills above Bern in Switzerland, Einstein asked his companion to imagine himself travelling on light beams from the various church clock towers they could see in the distance. What would the clock times show as they travelled away from them, they wondered? In that instant, Einstein realised that if the speed of light was fixed, time must be variable, and the rate of change of time must depend on the velocity of the observer. From this insight Einstein reasoned that energy and mass were also variables. This insight, and the famous equation that expressed it, signalled the beginning of the nuclear age.

Einstein's thought experiments are still the way students are taught the theory of relativity today. The story of how Einstein arrived at his discovery is what made the insight accessible to his peers (and anyone else determined to understand it). The story of an apple falling on Newton's head (which is probably a fiction, by the way) is how many generations of school children have learned about gravity. The story about the discovery is how we learn the discovery. Students remember the apple long after they've forgotten the inverse-square law of gravitational attraction. Teachers often don't appreciate this insight.

Whether changing the course of human history and winning a Nobel Prize or merely helping to avoid hiring the wrong salesperson, insights come in all shapes and sizes, but they are always a glorious, beautiful thing.

It's important not to jump into the insight story without having first made a connection, because we don't accept insights from people we don't know. Einstein was unknown when he published his 1905 papers, and his famous ideas languished until the Nobel Prize–winning physicist Max Planck read and appreciated them. The researcher's story helps us connect with the researcher and appreciate the insight. We start the insight story from common knowledge. Start where your client is and take them on the discovery journey. Then the insight makes sense because through the story they co-discover the insight with the researcher.

The story of how you got to the answer is not about how magnificent your idea or solution is; it's about how we arrived at this wonderful outcome. We all have a model of the world in our minds, but we need stories to expand our model step by step.

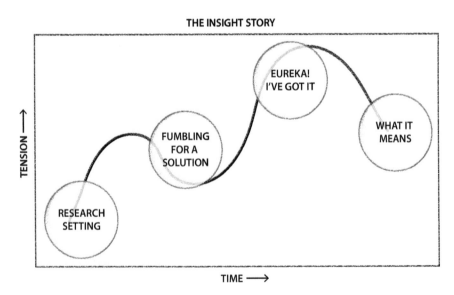

Figure 8.1: The researcher's journey — the insight story

Magicians, Marines and Medics

Some people think of 'business development' as a title on a business card that means they don't have to admit to being a salesperson, but someone who discovers and delivers insight is a true business developer. You'll hear the terms *hunter* and *farmer* to describe two basic sales types; hunters win new business and farmers nurture existing clients to grow the business within the account, so the thinking goes. I think it's more helpful to think of three funda-mental types of salespeople: I call them Magicians, Marines and Medics.

Magicians are the business development (BD) people. They find or create insight, and use that insight to formulate a sales pro-cess and open new markets. Marines are the foot soldiers who take insights and follow the process created by the Magician. Marines sell the same products and services, month after month, in a defined territory. This requires persistence, hard work and focus. Medics are the account managers who work to upsell existing customers and maintain the business relationship. The Medic's relationships and knowledge of the account are the keys to their success.

Business development magicians are brilliant at uncovering commercial insight, and they have the most critical need for it. Indeed, BD people are often more insightful about their clients' critical issues than their own company's marketing and product teams. They have the questioning, listening and coffee-drinking skills that other parts of the organisation lack. You drink a lot of coffee when you're in BD (other beverages may apply depending on your location).

Marines need insight prepared for them either by a Magician or by a market research team led by a sales leader. They need to be taught how to deliver the insight story and how to recognise a mobiliser in the customer organisation. We identify mobilisers in the customer organisation based on their reaction to the insight story (*Challenger Customer*, 2015).

Finding insight

Insight comes from shifting your focus away from your own company and solutions to your client's world. It is a paradox that a new salesperson can have an advantage in finding insight. When you are new you can ask dumb questions and get away with it. I think this explains how I have been able to step from one industry to another: I'm not scared to ask dumb questions.

When I went into the facility services industry I didn't understand much about my new company. I couldn't understand many of the internal conversations, but I spoke with the client anyway and asked them lots of questions. 'Tell me about your business.' 'Why do you do that?' 'Why are you spending twice the house value to refurbish it?'

When you look at their problems with fresh eyes, your questions will often prompt your client to stop and think differently too. Then you can advocate for them back in your own organisation. When you realise that there is no ready solution you start to search for insight. How do we look at their problem? Have we defined it correctly, or could there be different ways of looking at it? Could we combine different solutions? Do we need to partner with another company? How would you do it in a different industry? How might someone else do it? So the creativity begins.

By reading industry white papers and journals, and talking with your company's and your client's product development department, you can uncover important insights. Broadening your interests outside your own industry or geographical area can also lead to insights for your client. My example of adapting the government PPP business model for the resource industry is such a case. You are looking for similarities and analogies. It's truly a creative exercise. For me this is the most interesting and enjoyable part of selling, the true business development magician work. You're finding insights in your client's business and developing them in a way that creates something new for your client and your company—a unique advantage.

Can you always find an insight? I think you can. Most companies become set in their ways and internally focused. If you're willing to take an outsider view you will find insight, yet I've always found it to be a delightful surprise. Just remember to tell the story of that discovery.

Success stories: the hero's journey

Let's return for a deeper look at the second type of fight story, the success story. Where the insight story is told from the particular perspective of the researcher or your customer's customer, the success story is told from the perspective of your successful customer. You need to make your customer, not you or your company, the true hero of the story.

> **You need to make your customer, not you or your company, the true hero of the story.**

Joseph Campbell was an American mythologist who popularised comparative mythology and comparative religion. Campbell was fascinated by myths. He wanted to understand the elements of story and he was intrigued by the similarities in stories across cultures and religions. It was Campbell who first described the structure of the 'hero's journey' in detail. When you understand this universal story template you'll recognise it in many books and movies. Two famous movie examples are *The Karate Kid* and *Star Wars*. In *The Karate Kid*, the hero is a young boy who is bullied by a larger, stronger boy. The hero meets a master, who patiently trains him in the martial art of karate. Despite painful reverses, the hero ultimately defeats the bully in the tournament ring.

Campbell's original 1949[4] exposition of the 'monomyth' broke the hero's journey into seventeen stages. That's too many steps to remember, so I'm going to borrow from Donald Miller's simpler, seven-step framework from his excellent book *Building a Story Brand*.[5] In fact, I've cut it down to six steps for oral storytelling.

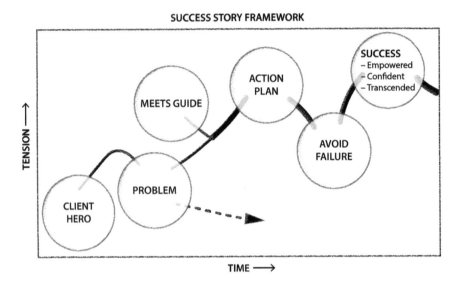

Figure 8.2: The six-event success story structure

It starts with the story hero (that's your client) in a stable, contented situation, before being forced to confront a new and difficult development. Along comes a guide[6] (your company), who presents a plan that calls the hero to action. The hero accepts the plan and follows through with it to avoid failure and achieve success. Here are the six steps (adapted from Donald's book) and how you might develop them:

1. **A hero.** Your client is situated in a setting with time and place markers.

2. **Has a problem.** Describe the event that characterises the problem.

3. **Meets a guide.** That is your company. Describe how the hero meets the guide.

4. **Who provides an action plan.** What was the plan proposed by your company? How does your hero react to the plan?

5. **Helps avoid failure.** What went wrong or could have gone wrong?

6. **Achieves success.** Describe the success. What was achieved? How does the hero feel now? How is the hero *transformed*?

The line arcing across the diagram in figure 8.1 represents the narrative arc of the story. The dotted line sloping down indicates the direction in which the hero was heading before the guide appeared to help out.

That's the hero's journey. It sounds simple enough, and it is if you follow this structure. But most vendors struggle to give up being the hero. You must understand that you're the guide. Last year when I set out to write this book I looked around for someone to help me and met Kath Walters. In our first meeting, I wanted to know about Kath's process. 'Are you a ghost writer?' I asked. 'No, I'm your Sherpa!' was Kath's reply. A wonderful metaphor that allowed me to see Kath as my guide. Metaphors, by the way, are 'stories on steroids'. This Sherpa 'story' was compressed into a sentence with imagery that provided instant illumination. Be the Sherpa for your clients.

As an aside, I should say that I'm not generally partial to guides, and I don't think I'm alone in this. I'm a do-it-yourself person. For example, I'm writing this book from an office that I built myself in our garage. But I knew that I was unlikely to complete a book unless I made an irreversible pre-commitment. Hiring Kath to be my Sherpa was that commitment, and she has been a wonderful guide!

Recognise you are your client's guide. Everyone who sells something must position themselves as the guide, because your client wants to be the hero who solves their own problems. That's the human condition: we all want to solve our own problems, but we'd like to have someone to help us out along the way. That's where you come in with your plan and call to action. And that's the structure of your success story. In a trite way, it's this:

Meet Luke Skywalker. Everything was going great, and now—oh shit!—he has a big problem. Princess Leah has been kidnapped. Luke meets a guide called Obi-Wan Kenobi (that's your company). Obi-Wan gives Luke access to the 'Force' (a plan). Luke isn't sure, but Obi-Wan is persistent. Luke almost fails (several times) but he has the 'Force' (our plan) and saves the day. There is always a moment of resistance when the guide meets the hero. That moment when the hero is trying to decide, 'Do I take a leap of faith, or do I just go my own way, the way I've always done things?'

Recognise you are the guide. Not the hero.

Let's look at an example from my business.

The financial wizard

One of our early clients was Jeff (not his real name), the part owner of a financial services company co-founded with his brother. Jeff invested a large sum of money in developing bespoke software and a business model to manage the financial affairs of high-net-worth individuals, people with a complex mix of business and personal finances.

After a few years of development, the software finally worked, but Jeff couldn't attract and convert enough new clients. There was a serious risk the investment would be a complete financial loss. And Jeff's inability to find new clients was causing strain in his relationship with his brother. His brother was CEO and had always been considered the 'salesperson' of the team. But the new service and software was Jeff's baby. Jeff had to sell it but selling was way out of his comfort zone as one trained as an accountant.

Jeff came to us in 2014 and asked us to review his business development approach. We assessed his methodology and I gave him a sales conversation screening test. To say Jeff's approach was lacking is a huge understatement. He was 100 percent analytical, relying on long-winded technical emails to approach new clients. On the rare occasion he secured a meeting he spent 95 percent of the time talking. The concepts of building rapport and consulting with questions seemed to be unknown to Jeff.

My first inclination was to propose he hire a salesperson. I didn't think Jeff could succeed at sales. He was open to that idea but insisted we first train him to sell. He was determined to prove to himself he could do it.

The development plan created for Jeff included individual coaching on telephone calling and consultative meetings. We taught questioning, listening and story skills. Jeff is the best student I've had in twenty years of helping salespeople. He followed the plan to the letter. He devoured everything we gave him, practised relentlessly and slowly started to win business. He was motivated. As he gained customers we helped him obtain testimonials and success stories, and his clients became raving fans.

Then, calamity. There was an acrimonious falling out with his brother. For several months they fought, eventually agreeing to go their separate ways. Jeff would take over the business, the staff and the new software code and manage on his own.

But Jeff was a changed man. Gone was the lack of confidence and fear of failure. Now he knows how to sell and how to deliver value to his clients. He's doing well on his own, master of his own destiny.

Let's analyse the story. First, note that it's a story about Jeff. It's not about our consulting company, although as his guide we have a part to play.

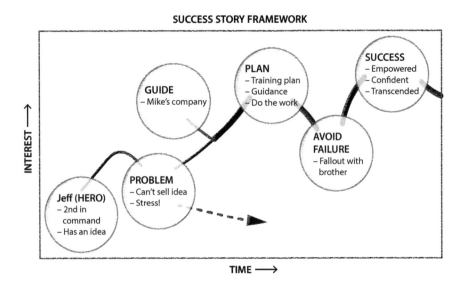

Figure 8.3: Jeff's success journey

We trace Jeff's story from his struggle with sales and struggles with his brother to finding a guide and building his skills and confidence through dedicated action. On the journey he is tested by the split with his brother. Finally, he transcends the problem. He is a new person with new powers. That's the hero's journey. It takes just over two minutes to tell.

A great way to think of yourself in your sales career is, 'I am someone that helps my client create their stories'. You will help curate their story.

> **A salesperson: Someone who helps their client create their own success story.**

Future success stories

There is a type of success story in which the success hasn't yet happened. I call these 'a day in your future life stories'. Rather than tell about another client who has achieved success with your help, you tell a story about how your client's life will be after receiving the benefits of your products and services. The 'Prague Play' story in chapter 1 is an example.

The future success story is a useful technique if you have a new offering and no history of success, and you should use the same success story structure, the hero's journey. Of course, your client will know 'it's just a story', but you will still help them experience the benefits of your offering in their mind before they purchase. It's not ideal, but sometimes it's the best you can do!

The failure story

A failure story is not the opposite of a success story. In fact, personal failure stories can be turned into success stories with just one additional line: '… and I'll never do that again!' or 'and that's how I learned to …'

A story about the failure of one of your clients, or a competitor's client, is a more sensitive matter, however. I encourage you to find stories that turn out well for your client hero or you run the risk of the story seeming like gossip. Good success stories do often linger on the mishaps, near misses and potential for catastrophe, but they must be resolved so they end up in a safe positive place.

Now you understand about insight and success stories, it's time to learn how to develop your own stories so you can fight like a champion.

9. The fight for your customer's mind

I feel I change my mind all the time. And I sort of feel that's your responsibility as a person, as a human being — to constantly be updating your positions on as many things as possible.

Malcolm Gladwell, Canadian author

Your fish is on the line, twisting and turning. You reel in with a story then let the line run so the story finds its place. Developing your insight and success stories requires creativity and effort, but the payoff is huge. You're going to be the only option in many more situations. You'll win more deals and command higher prices. How will you find these two stories? Let's look at insight stories first.

Of course it depends on your situation. Perhaps your company is bringing out a new product; they've done good market research and have developed a commercial insight. It still needs to be put in the form of a story, which is something your marketing research people may not appreciate. Often they'll provide pie charts, tables, graphs and hundreds of slides — but no story. If there is a good insight, you'll think, *That's fabulous, because my clients don't know about that*, but you need to find the story about how the insight was found. Go to the source. Who did this work? Ask to speak with them.

When you've found the lead researcher, interview them to get the insight story. Start with the setting. When and where did they discover the insight? Then backtrack for the backstory. How did they get into this field? What's their personal story? Delve into the insight discovery. What was the methodology? Where did they start? What were the working hypotheses? It's a surprising result, so how did they find it? When you've got the bones of the story, ask about their emotions. How did they feel during the process? Were they surprised? Did people believe the results, or was there resistance? You're trying to capture the highs and lows of a typical research project, because no one ever finds commercial insight without going through pain and effort. You're looking for the story behind the facts they've delivered.

This is the easy route to the insight story. The hard way is finding the insight yourself. You'll be the story. I've done this myself several times when I've had the business development magician role. I'm not sure everyone has this ability. You must have a curious mind. It starts with conversations with the client, and the less infected your mind is with details of your company's products and services, the better these conversations go.

The curse of knowledge

A barrier to finding insight is the 'curse of knowledge' problem.[1] When you know a lot about a subject it's easy to make unwarranted assumptions about other people's capacity to understand you. You also tend to assume that you've seen every buyer situation and stop treating each buyer as unique. There is a 'hump' curve effect. It usually takes a while — maybe a year — for a salesperson selling complex products and services to become an effective seller. They're not selling well to start off with because there's a lot to learn. Then they get effective, and they do well for a year or so. Then their performance drops off. It's a common pattern.[2] At the heart of why their sales results drop is 'vendor-speak'—they start talking the internal language of their products and services and they assume that they've heard every type of client problem. They forget how to talk to their client with a curious mind as they did, when they started in the role.

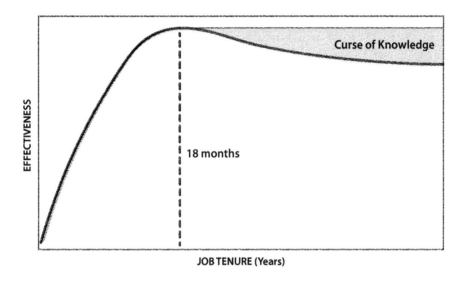

Figure 9.1: The sales effectiveness 'hump curve' effect

So you have only a short period of effectiveness, unless you notice the pattern and train yourself to preserve your curious mind and to be open in the way you look at client problems. Not making assumptions, not thinking you have the answer—these are key.

It starts with asking your client about how and why they do their business the way they do and listening with the sole intent of understanding what is said. If you do this well and the client trusts your intent, you can move on to deeper questions. Questions about what doesn't work well for them. What's a challenge? Why is that? What have they been doing themselves to fix it? Why haven't they fixed it? This type of deep questioning comes from a state of curiosity and humility and only proceeds with trust. You must first have made the connection.

It's difficult to describe what happens in this type of exploration discussion. You're allowing your mind to do what it does — to look for and sift through analogies to find the insight. I think that's what insight actually is: the elusive analogy. A prediction that ties your customer's issue to a solution possibility. The analogy links back to what you already know but lets you see it from a new perspective.

You can't rush it. Companies maintain research departments because they're trying to find insight. It's an expensive, time-consuming process. Keep in mind your client knows all about their world and your company knows all about its world. It's the white space in between that you focus on. It's useful to think of yourself as the liaison or bridge between the two companies. You live in that space between the two organisations.

The insight discovery story

The standard market research approach is to synthesise and summarise research into new facts. In doing so, they forget they've had the benefit of the research process to understand those facts. Your client won't have had that advantage. If it wasn't you who found the insight, it's your job to tell the insight discovery story. In my example with the PPP, I told my mining client the story about meeting with my company's business development department and being surprised to find they were working on a similar problem with a radically different solution. I took my mining company client on my personal journey of finding the insight. In that example, I was the researcher.

The insight discovery story uses the simple story structure. As introduced in Part 1, it's a four-part story, with setting (with a time and a place), some complications, a turning point and a resolution, which is the insight. We follow the journey of the insight discoverer.

INSIGHT STORY—STEPS AND QUESTIONS

How was the insight discovered?

Who was the researcher(s)/discoverer?

Can you interview them? (Do so if you can.)

What were they doing just before the insight?

Find out about their background—schooling etc.

Was the insight discovery a deliberate process?

Or serendipity?

Describe the exact moment when the insight became apparent.

How did you feel?

What did you do then?

Has the insight changed your life? How?

How should the insight be packaged and delivered?

Is the insight unique?

Figure 9.2: Insight story cheat sheet

Once you've got your story, it's tempting to run and tell it to your client, but I suggest you tell it first to yourself, to the mirror or to video and then internally to see how people receive it. With each telling you refine and practise it. Stories are too long when you first tell them. They start out five, six, seven minutes long and your client's eyes will glaze over before the end. You can relay the same message with more impact in a one- to two-minute story that really hits home, but only if you do a few practice iterations.

Is your insight story good enough?

What if you tell your story and it bombs? It will do so for one of two reasons: either the insight wasn't actually very insightful, or your story misses crucial technical points. Maybe it doesn't start with a time and place, or fails to show vulnerability and complications, or has the wrong hero perspective, or doesn't make a business point. Step through these possibilities to work out the reason the story failed. You'll know if it's a good story, because when you practise it someone will go, 'Wow!' We feel a good story in our gut and in our heart. We have an emotional reaction to it. If you're not getting this sort of response to your story, keep working on it.

What if it's not a useful insight? Sometimes we build in our own minds what we think is an amazing insight and the client says, 'I already know that,' or they explain why it wouldn't work. Then it's back to the drawing board. We must have a quality insight. But when we find it, one insight story can build an entire business. The Xerox colour copier story could be a multi-billion-dollar story. One story. So don't be discouraged if at first it's not the right insight. Keep working at it. Sometimes you'll find a brilliant insight but it's not unique. Your company doesn't have unique rights to the insight.

Network scheming

When I joined Siemens, in 2003, my role was to get my major telecommunications client to buy our new mobile network equipment. It was a most difficult task because there were many competitors and my client was joined at the hip to our major competitor. For twenty years their favourite supplier had supplied them with mobile network equipment. At that time my client operated three different types of networks, which was a complex undertaking. Their competitors had only one type of network to operate. My client knew they needed to migrate to a fourth, more modern type of network, which at the time was 3G. We sold 3G networks but so did their favourite supplier and at least five other companies. So why us? To me, we seemed to be one of the least suitable suppliers.

New to the industry, I didn't know much about my client's business or our technology, but I spent time with one of their network managers who was willing to answer my questions about multiple networks and the difficulties and costs of managing them in an integrated way. I scoured the world for other Siemens customers in a similar situation and found a solution to the multiple networks problem by combining two ideas. In the United States we were delivering a particular type of 3G network that, if modified in a way that had already been done by one of our competitors, would allow my client to retire their old networks. Siemens had a key component of that solution in the United States.

I had an insight. It was a brilliant solution to a critical problem, and neither my client nor any of my competitors knew about it.

Was my insight good enough, though? I met with senior management in the client company and told two stories that together showed how we could eliminate three networks and replace them with one new network. They loved the idea. They were captivated by it. Our major competitor, the 'favourite supplier', hadn't thought of this solution.

In that instant, I had provided my client with insight of incredible value. But the perfect insight would have been something none of my competitors could do. My major competitor could take our idea. Worse, my company had a major delivery failure in the United States and we blew our credibility with my client's senior management team. Our competitor took my insight and developed it into a new, multi-billion-dollar network.

This story shows that you can have a fantastic insight story and still not win. It's never a sure thing, but you're lifting your chances. Before delivering that insight, we were in a melee with six other suppliers, and not even in the conversation. With that insight, for a few weeks we were the front runner. We just didn't get it over the line.

Collecting success stories

Success stories are easier than insight stories. If you've been in business for a while, you'll have many of them. Success stories are routinely created when you run a good business, but most business people don't collect them in the right way. Or they don't collect them at all.

How do we collect success stories? By asking our operations people and our customer service people which clients have had a good experience. Which ones stand out as interesting situations? Then we go and have a chat with the client or talk with them on the phone. 'Why are you happy? Why did you choose us? What was your decision-making process? Why us and not them? What went right? What went wrong? How did you feel before the purchase? And after the implementation?' The answers to those questions, along with the basic situation information, provides us with the material for a success story that we can tell in a minute or two.

Who on the client side was the main buyer? Who will be the main character of your story? Why did they buy, and who implemented it? You may need to interview a few people. As I changed industries, I was amazed to observe how rarely these conversations take place. That's a huge lost opportunity. I had a mining client spending $60 million a year with us, and no one in my company could tell me why they bought our services. They had a few vague ideas, but when I interviewed the client I found that those ideas were wrong. The real reasons for the purchase were surprising.

SUCCESS STORY—STEPS AND QUESTIONS

Who is the client hero of this story?

Can I interview them? (If yes, do so.)

Who else knows about the success?

Where and when did it happen?

What were the conditions before the success journey?

What options were considered?

What would have happened if there had been no success journey?

What would have been the impact of this?

Did the client have doubts about the new solution?

What did they fear?

How did the success journey go? Were there missteps?

What are you most proud of now?

How do you feel now?

What has been the result? Can you quantify it?

How has it changed you?

Who has been affected by the result?

How does the future look now?

What would you say to others in your position before the success project?

Figure 9.3: Success story cheat sheet

If you chase a piece of business and lose, it's not easy to find the true reason for losing. Your lost customer is busy implementing the project with your competitor. You're likely to get a cursory, face-saving answer such as, 'Your price was too high'. When you win the business, though, you have easy access to a client who would like to be open and helpful. So why not ask why you won? There's no reason not to ask, but it seems most suppliers don't. Or they fail to listen carefully to the answer.

One of the services I provide for my consulting clients is to make a 'testimonial call' to their best customers. I often glean excellent success stories from these calls. It's a straightforward process that I learned from Alex Goldfayn's excellent book *The Revenue Growth Habit*.[3] I ask my client for the names of their best customers. My client sends an email introducing me and letting them know that I'd like to give them a call and talk to them about my client's service. I'm doing a few of these as I draft this book.

In the previous chapter, I told you about Jeff, the 'financial wizard' owner of a financial services company. Jeff's clients have a complex mix of personal and business finances, and Jeff does a great job managing their finances.

Jeff's critical issue is gaining trust. The first thing he needs when he meets prospective clients is access to all their personal and business financial information so he can estimate how much money he can save them. That's a massive trust issue! How does he get new clients when his first ask is such a confidential matter? Jeff has struggled to build his business for this reason. He is brilliant at what he does, but getting new clients is extremely difficult.

Jeff needed success stories, testimonials and existing clients willing to refer him. I explained the testimonial call process and eventually called eleven of his clients on his behalf. Jeff was nervous about possible negative comments from these calls, but his clients were uniformly delighted with his service and happy to talk about their experience! He was amazed at how positive their comments were.

I asked Jeff's clients, 'Tell me, how were you able to trust someone you didn't know? Why did you hand over your financial information? What steps did you take to ensure it was safe?' They told me all the things they did to satisfy themselves that Jeff could be trusted. In the process, they told me the stories that Jeff's new clients needed to hear. These are beautiful success stories. I typically talked on the phone for ten to fifteen minutes and I got ten to fifteen testimonials and a success story. At the end of each call I asked them if it would be okay for Jeff to use some of their comments in his marketing. In every case I got, not 'Okay', but 'Yes, please do! And if I can help Jeff by talking with one of his potential clients, I'm happy to do so.' Eleven testimonial calls yielded more than 120 testimonials, 11 stories and 11 clients willing to assist with Jeff's business development and some referrals. Not bad for a couple of hours of telephone calls.

During the call I asked the types of questions that salespeople are (hopefully) trained to ask: 'Could you tell me about the situation when you first met Jeff? How did you start with his services? What's been good about the service? What has that meant for you? What has been the impact on you personally and on your business? Please describe the journey from when you first met him.' With these types questions you prompt them to talk. My success rate is 100 percent. They all say flattering things, they all tell an interesting story and they all agree to their comments being used for marketing purposes.

Why do people agree to answer these questions? They like being recognised as a good client, as special, and they already have an affinity with your business. I find it interesting that most business people don't appreciate how much their clients like them. I suspect it may be because your clients contact you when they need something or to complain when something isn't working. They don't contact you to say how much they enjoy your service, so you get a skewed understanding of their attitude towards your business.

More important than the testimonials and success stories, customers who publicly acknowledge the benefits of your services have been converted into even bigger fans, with massive future potential.

The reference manual of sales persuasion is Robert Cialdini's 1984 book *Influence: The Psychology of Persuasion*. Cialdini identifies six fundamental principles of persuasion:

- **Reciprocity.** I give you something and you feel obligated to give me something in return.

- **Social proof.** You should do this because everyone else is doing it.

- **Authority.** This authority figure says you should do this.

- **Liking.** I like you so I'll do what you say.

- **Scarcity.** Buy now or you will miss out.

- **Commitment to consistency.** If I help you once, I'll help you again—to be consistent as someone who helps you.

That final principle of commitment to consistency is the one most people struggle to appreciate. Though it is not well understood, it can play a huge part in your sales success. Let's look at it in context.

Cialdini and the commitment experiment

Cialdini describes a psychology experiment that illustrates the commitment to consistency principle.[4] In the 1960s a researcher posing as a volunteer went door to door in a suburban neighbourhood in Los Angeles. The volunteer asked homeowners to support a community road safety initiative by allowing a billboard to be erected on their front lawn. Homeowners were shown a picture of an attractive house obscured by a huge billboard with the poorly lettered words DRIVE CAREFULLY. Understandably, the request success rate was low. However, one group of householders agreed at a rate of 76 percent! Two weeks earlier those households had made a small commitment to road safety by agreeing to place a discreet road safety sign on their front door. Incredibly, most householders who had agreed to the small sign also agreed to the billboard request.

The reason for the compliance change is that while displaying the road safety sign the householder began to identify with that community cause. Maybe a neighbour or friend asked about the sticker, and they responded, 'Yes, I support road safety awareness.' They were *primed* to comply with the billboard request. If you get someone to give you a small thing, they'll probably give you a bigger thing, and that's a powerful principle in persuasion. If you get a customer to agree to the testimonial call and they say nice things about your service, it strengthens their connection with you. They identify as a supporter of your business and because of the principle of consistency they are more likely to agree to a subsequent larger request. They may even agree to speak at a customer forum on your behalf, or do a video testimonial for your website — things they would not do without a prior commitment to your company.

If you look only inside your own organisation, success stories often won't turn out so well. You'll get the list of potential stories from within your company, but you then need to go to those clients and get the story first-hand so you can tell it from their perspective. You may not be able to or want to mention the success client's real name. In my financial services example, future clients are not going to feel comfortable if they think you've compromised the privacy of an existing client by naming them in a story. It's easy to anonymise the story, though. You can say, 'I have a client in a situation like yours, we'll call her Wendy,' then tell Wendy's story. It will still be an authentic story because of the descriptive details and emotions you include without divulging the identity of your client. Anonymity is fine but it has to be a real story about a specific situation that actually happened.

Another way to uncover success stories is to facilitate a story workshop with a group of sales, operations and customer service staff. I do this with most of my clients. In a day or a half day we teach them what stories are and get them telling success stories from their experience. They usually tell these stories from their own perspective, but that's okay. They get practice telling a story and you get a list of customers to follow up with. A story workshop is a motivating event because the best stories reside only in the minds of the founders and the very best salespeople. The workshop gets these stories out and into the minds of everyone in the sales team.

The final step after a story workshop is to capture the stories in either written or video form. Give each story a memorable name and picture, and post them in your story library. Every sales team needs a library for its stories and other persuasion collateral such as testimonials, scripts and sample meeting conversations.

> **Every sales team needs a library for its stories and other persuasion collateral such as testimonials, scripts and sample meeting conversations.**

You may be wondering whether you have an obligation to go back to the client and show them the story. At my company, our stories are posted in a public story library, so I do send the story for review and ask for permission. They say, 'Great.' They don't mind. I let them know as a courtesy so they know it's published and in case someone asks them about it. Your story library is likely to be internal and confidential, so you don't need to be too concerned about client approval or the quality of production. Quick videos shot on a smartphone are fine as long as the sound quality is good.

Delivering a success story

A well-honed success story takes only a minute or two to deliver. They are short and get shorter as you practise them. We normally don't use the word 'story' when delivering the story because some people still associate it with a fabrication or something childish. Don't say, 'I'm going to tell you a story', but rather, 'That reminds me of ... [when I was in this situation ... a client just like you ...].' Or you could say, 'I'd like to make a point about system main-tenance. I had a client just like you in this situation.'

Sometimes the story is humorous, a good pub story, but wouldn't work as a client success story, like the 'skinning a cat' story I told in chapter 2. Try to imagine how your future client will receive your story. Are you telling it for your benefit or theirs?

You've hooked your fish and now you're fighting to keep it on the line. The fight stories — insight and success — are the essence of successful selling. For me they are the heart of sales. Do I come to my client with a valuable insight? Am I able to get them to appreciate it? Can my success story persuade them to live that insight and want to act on it? If I can do that, I'm a salesperson.

You've done a brilliant job! You've connected and delivered insight. They get it, but they still have to sign on the dotted line. You're not finished. You have fought hard for this deal and you've helped them to believe in your solution — they can taste it. What a disaster it would be if it slipped away now! What a massive loss of potential. Losing would hurt badly when you have put in this level of effort. Let's move on to a champagne ending for you and your client. In Part 4 we put stories to work to land your big fish.

Winning the fight checklist

✓ What unique insight do you have about your customer's business? Tell the story of how you discovered that insight.

✓ Do you have customers who have succeeded by using your products and services? Then tell their stories.

✓ Upload your insight and values stories to your story library so everyone in the team can fight with them.

Part 4

LAND

Landing the Deal

In this part:

Values stories

Sales teaching stories

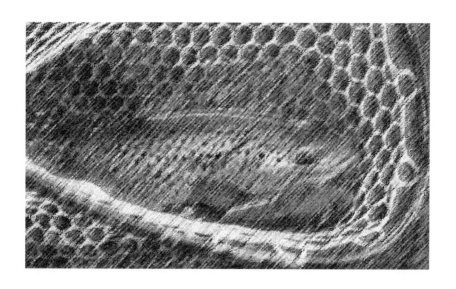

10. I submitted the proposal—now what?

In our age there is no such thing as keeping out of politics.
All issues are political issues, and politics itself is a mass
of lies, evasions, folly, hatred and schizophrenia.

George Orwell, British author

Imagine how easy selling would be if you knew exactly what was happening with your future customer, if you could read your customer's mind?

Hell's Gateway: A failure story

In the mid 2000s, I was a new account executive for an international technology conglomerate and we were invited to tender for a network subsystem for a large telecommunications company.

I had no idea whether our company could compete, but I figured our chances were slim because our main competitors already supplied equipment in the customer's network. They had relationships and experience. We did not.

My knowledge of the specific technology was nonexistent, but I downloaded the 150-slide PowerPoint deck (!) and was pleasantly surprised to find that we were credible. We'd had success delivering that technology all over the world. Our senior management were keen to bid.

It was an expensive tender to prepare, requiring several months of effort by technical experts in Europe, Asia and Australia. After submission, international experts were flown in for presentations and everyone was hopeful for what would be a deal worth several tens of millions.

A couple of weeks later we made the shortlist and were hit with a barrage of clarification requests. Good news!

And then… nothing.

Then… more nothing.

Calls to the procurement office were met with a polite 'We're still in the evaluation phase'. Our management was getting nervous. 'Maybe we should drop the price?' my boss suggested.

'But we have no way of knowing whether price is an issue.' I said.

'Well, it can't hurt…' was the reply. (*It won't help*, was my unspoken response.)

We unilaterally dropped our price, twice! By more than a million dollars. Still no response. Four months later, we received a one-paragraph message informing us our bid was unsuccessful.

I met with the customer's technical lead to find out what had happened. Our two competitors were the customer's main equipment supplier of other network systems (let's call them Big Supplier) and a niche company (Little Supplier), which had supplied the subsystem being replaced. Little Supplier was not well regarded for service and operational reasons, and there was a clear intention to replace them. Big Supplier did not have a fully compliant solution. Our solution was considered the best overall fit by the customer's scoring system, taking all factors into consideration. Full compliance and ease of systems integration (not price!) were the key scoring factors.

Why didn't we win if we scored highest? Here is what happened.

After the tender submission, Big Supplier engaged in a negotiation wider than the tender scope, and the customer saw an opportunity for savings in other parts of their network. Eventually those negotiations broke down. By then Little Supplier's contract was expiring and there wasn't enough time to proceed with any other supplier. So the least preferred incumbent, Little Supplier, won the deal.

That's a sales failure story.

It was my responsibility to know what was going on and I was mostly clueless. I didn't even know that the customer had a high opinion of our technology and wanted us in their network.

Like a general in wartime, you normally don't have the full picture in a sales engagement. If you did, the job would be easy. Nonetheless there are stories that could have helped me win that deal.

The point of this story, and this last part of the book, is that you must continue to influence your buyer after you've submitted a proposal or tender. Otherwise all your good work connecting with hook stories and differentiating with fight stories is at risk.

As you'll see, the advice in these chapters applies especially to larger B2B deals. The types of stories you can use are valid for all deal sizes, but they're particularly useful when you need to close large deals. That's because the larger the deal, the more people are likely to be involved in the decision and the less visibility you have of the decision process.

You probably won't get a chance to meet many of those people, simply because of the size and structure of the organisations you'll be dealing with. That means there will be decision makers, and in particular veto decision makers, you won't know who can stop your deal. That's difficult to manage, and one of the few tools you have at your disposal is stories designed to work in these situations—land stories.

Why deals don't get done

When I meet with business owners and sales leaders, we talk about all sorts of issues they have with their sales and sales teams. In general, these issues fall into two categories:

1. Their salespeople can't open or can't get enough prospects.

2. Their salespeople can't close.

Put those two things together and it adds up to 'they can't sell'. Curiously, sales leaders don't mention the third problem, which is that their team can't differentiate their company's products and services. That seems to be a widely unacknowledged problem. We talked about the 'can't open' problem in the Hook phase of the book. Our insight and success stories in the Fight phase are a bridge to the closing problem. We've used stories to get us to the landing, but closing deals is a tough task for salespeople and sales leaders.

Salespeople are expensive and if they spend time on deals that don't lead to business, that's a complete waste of company money. It's a double blow when you lose. You waste company resources and your winning competitor becomes stronger. You're in a worse situation than before you decided to chase the deal.

One cause of failure to close is the stagnant pipeline problem. Deals that sit in the pipeline and aren't closed are a critical issue. The longer they sit there, the less likely they'll close. It's instructive to watch the excitement for a deal evaporate as the landing phase approaches. The salespeople are mentally spending their sales commission check. They make a proposal or answer a tender ... then nothing happens. Excitement fades into despair. Why is this? The reason is that while they were meeting the client, before the proposal stage, the client wasn't thinking about *making a difficult decision.*

In the Hook and Fight stages your future client is in a different mind space, happily imagining the future benefits of change. Now in the Land phase they have to make a decision, and that's when they think about risks rather than benefits. Will I lose my job with this decision? Is this really the thing we should be spending our money on? Should we spend our precious resources on something else? These risk discussions are typically done in groups of four, five, six people. A financial person might be involved, a project manager, an operations manager, business managers. People with different functional responsibilities get together to come to an agreement. Each has different ideas about what should be a priority, but as a group they know they're taking a risk when they're spending money to make a change.

That's one of the main reasons deals don't get done. They die in the pipeline because people are risk averse. The Land phase is the crucial step in sales. It's the money play. Businesses fail if they can't get the deal done. It's the crux of being a salesperson. Can I get this deal done, yes or no? This hasn't changed in the thirty-plus years I've been in business. If anything is different now it's that buyers think they're more informed than they really are, because they can hop on the internet and access any kind of information. But they're also more confused than ever. They're paralysed by the different options brought on by rapid technological change.

Deals die in the pipeline because people are risk averse.

With technology changing so rapidly, why make a decision now? Why not wait for the next big thing that's going to solve my problem? Decision making becomes more challenging when buyers have greater access to rapidly changing information.

The stories you're going to learn in this part are about short-circuiting decision paralysis. They will give you a tool to help allay the fears of the decision committee and get the deal over the line. When you understand and use these stories you'll close more deals. The benefit of having a set of tools that will systematically get your deals closed faster is incalculable. It's a wonderful thing. I'm also going to teach you how to deploy these stories through a sales team so you can systematically improve the team's performance at this stage of the sales cycle.

Let's go back to my story of selling the network system to a large telecommunications company, my 'Hell's Gateway' sales failure story at the beginning of the chapter. You were probably thinking, I was just a poor salesperson because I didn't understand the client's situation well enough or position our product properly. What has that got to do with stories? The answer is in the details.

After we found out we had lost the deal I arranged a meeting with the client's technical sponsor.

When I met Wayne, we instantly connected because we shared a sense of frustration. He was frustrated with his own company, and with himself for not being able to navigate the internal politics to get a sensible decision (to buy my company's products and services). I was frustrated with months of not knowing what was happening during the stalled decision phase, then discovering we had lost the deal.

The emotion we had in common was a connecting point and we shared our stories. We became friends. I still keep in touch with him. He's living up on the Gold Coast now and has worked for three different companies since we first met. The first lesson from this story is that I connected with my buyer *after* the deal instead of before it! Tony Hughes, sales author and prolific sales blogger, says, 'The way we open largely determines the probability of a successful close.' He's right.

Suppose we had properly connected before the deal? Wayne was stymied by his decision team's infighting, which led to a decision he felt was not in the company's best interests. How could I have helped him? That's what we'll talk about in this part.

When I reviewed that lost opportunity, I resolved to change my approach in a couple of ways. The first was always to establish a proper connection in any deal I work on. If I can't get the connection, I'm not proceeding with the deal. The second resolution was that I must help my future client to achieve their outcome in complex political situations such as the one Wayne was in. I had to help him because he didn't have the skills to persuade his buying committee. Wayne didn't know how to influence his organisation to get a sensible result. He couldn't do it on his own; he needed coaching on persuasion. What is the one skillset that sellers have that buyers lack? Sales skills, of course!

What is the one skillset that sellers have that buyers lack? Sales skills.

So there are two failures in this story: the failure to connect and the failure to coach in the blackout period when Wayne needed to influence his own decision-making team. I left him hanging out to dry.

Wayne could see the train wreck happening in his company but he couldn't create the emotion within the buying committee to motivate change. He needed a sales teaching story—specifically, a cost-of-delay story to create urgency. Cost of delay is one of a suite of stories that I group in the category of Sales Teaching Stories.

The other issue for Wayne was that the decision committee wasted so much time that the only 'risk-free' option seemed to be to remain with Little Supplier. In fact, there was plenty of time, but the committee became increasingly risk averse. Our company had a tremendous capacity to move heaven and earth for a client in difficulty. It's part of our corporate values. If I'd armed Wayne with a story that illustrated this value of delivery he would have been more persuasive. Values stories and teaching stories were the two persuasion tools that Wayne lacked. When I contacted Wayne to check his memory of events for this book, he described that project as 'a tale of interference, indecision and corporate inertia at its finest'.

What's the conventional wisdom on closing?

The conventional wisdom on what to do during the Land phase is contained within that failure story. Badger the client for details about what's happening, answer all the clarification requests and unilaterally drop your price. This happens more often than you might think. As you can see in this story, dropping the price was the wrong thing to do. It couldn't influence the decision; it just made us look desperate.

There are other approaches to closing the deal. Type 'closing the deal' into YouTube or Google and you'll get thousands of hits on what I call 'one-shot tricks'. There are library shelves of books on the subject. One of America's most famous salespeople and sales trainers, Zig Ziglar, wrote a book called *Zig Ziglar's Secrets of Closing the Sale* (1984). It contains more than 100 closing tricks, including the famous 'Alternative Choice Close'[1]: 'Would you like it delivered to your warehouse or to your office?' These tricks were debunked for large-deal B2B closing by Neil Rackham in his 1988 book *SPIN Selling*[2], based on research from 35,000 sales calls over 12 years. Rackham tells the story of observing a sales guy trying the alternate choice close on a seasoned procurement professional. The response was, 'Would you like me to throw you out, or would you like me to get security to do it?'[3] Tricks to get people to say yes then and there are worthless when the decision is being made by a committee you don't meet.

I have seen some oddball approaches to the Land phase. Here's one of my favourites.

The art exhibition ploy

In the early 2000s, before he became my sales manager, Paul Thompson was sweating over the result of a major tender. It was the 'radio silence' period, when the customer's tender rules precluded contact. Paul was nervous about the result and wanted to continue influencing the decision process.

He found out that his customer didn't own their corporate HQ building and arranged with the building owner to sponsor an art exhibition in the main lobby. The tender evaluation team would pass his company's advertising each day as they walked through the exhibition in their foyer.

Paul happened to be attending the art exhibition when the customer's head of procurement walked past. He looked at Paul with a smile and shook his finger as if to say, 'Never again.' Paul won that tender, and the customer's tender rules now preclude that practice!

Paul is an exceptionally creative salesman. A commoner approach to the Land phase is simply waiting, fingernail biting. Vendors put everything (and I mean everything) into the response document and hope it speaks for itself. 'If we win, we win; if we lose, we lose,' they say philosophically. That's great. If you favour that approach, I'd like to have you as my sales competitor. Because there's still a lot you can do after you've submitted the proposal.

Your success will depend on the earlier stages, on the work you put into the Hook and Fight stages. It also depends on helping your sponsor fight your case in the decision committee, and that is what we will focus on now.

Remember, your sponsor is the person in the client decision committee who wants you as their supplier. This sponsor may be a technical leader or a business owner. They may also be the financial owner who believes your solution offers the best financial features. If you don't have a sponsor, you're probably not going to win the deal.

Your tools in the Land stage are *values stories* and *sales teaching stories*, and of course, the retelling of your insight and success stories. If those are strong stories, they'll be retold and continue to work for you in the decision phase. Values and teaching stories will do even more to turn the decision your way.

What I'm talking about here is not well known or understood. The best salespeople often tell these stories unwittingly. They're unconsciously competent storytellers who get great results. Consequently there's not much written about it. I find it interesting that great salespeople turned authors, like Zig Ziglar, don't discuss storytelling as a sales technique, yet their books are crammed full of fascinating stories. That's what makes these books so compelling. Somehow, Ziglar didn't join the dots to connect his storytelling skill with his sales skill and describe his storytelling techniques, which are formidable.

People follow the conventional wisdom because that's what they've seen other people do. The conventional wisdom in sales works some of the time, because buyers have to buy! That doesn't mean the salesperson necessarily used the best (or even a good) technique. The fact that your buyer bought doesn't mean you're a good salesperson. That's a tough lesson in self-awareness for salespeople.

The stress reliever

By tapping into the power of persuasive stories you will allay the feeling of risk your buyer has, help them to choose you in their decision process, and get them focused on the benefits they're going to enjoy from using your products and solutions. It gives you a winning edge.

Mastering and deploying the land stories gives sales organisations concrete things to do in what is otherwise a high-stress waiting game. What salespeople normally do when a big decision is in the balance is get anxious. I've been there. You can still stress, if you like, but be practical and deploy your stories.

You want your client champion to know the land stories for their decision-meeting conversations. You may not know what risks are coming up and what decision blocks will occur until you're in this phase, so flexibility and a good backdoor communication channel with your client sponsor are key.

When you submit your tender or proposal, your client may seek to reassure you: 'Everything is okay. We like your company, and we want your products and solutions.' But if your client is unfamiliar with buying your type of solution, risks and doubts are exposed and decision barriers will pop up.

If you have built a good relationship in the Hook stage, you'll be told about decision issues even in a formal tender. They'll want to tell you what's going on because you're friends and they trust you. When we understand what the decision problem is, what the specific fears and risks are, then we can tell the appropriate story. Perhaps it's a values story to allay fears and uncertainties or a teaching story to overcome consensus issues.

Of course, storytelling doesn't absolve you of responsibility for asking astute questions, for really understanding the situation and proposing a high-value solution. Storytelling is a persuasion tool that must work in parallel with other aspects of good salesmanship[4] and good 'solutioning'.

Hook and fight stories can be created and used by any salesperson, indeed any person who interacts with your clients, but land stories are the domain of people with significant experience of deal-making. Often the values stories, which I'll talk more about in the next chapters, are created and triggered by leaders in your organisation. The sales teaching stories are invariably told by people with deep experience in closing similar types of deals.

There are two information-gathering steps you need to take before preparing land stories:

1. Discuss with your client the risks they see in your solution. What do they not want to happen? Ideally you should have this conversation with every member of the decision committee. Alternatively, ask your sponsor to tell you about each member of the committee and their main concerns. Ask about both business and personal risks and fears.

2. Talk with your client sponsor about their decision process and how they reach agreement. Can they anticipate any potential blocks?

With the information drawn from these conversations you can prepare stories that will guide them through the decision-making process. This is especially important if your future customer has never bought anything like your solution before. Who knows what things can go wrong when buying your products and services? You do. You must find stories around the closing process from past clients who have been through the process. This gives your client the confidence to proceed.

Finally, it's very important while landing the deal to keep telling the insight and success stories that you developed during the Fight stage. They will continue to work for you. Reminding your sponsor of those stories and suggesting they retell them in their internal meetings is a great piece of coaching.

The deal isn't done until the contract is signed. You must continue to influence all the way through the decision process, and land stories will do this work for you, even when you're not there. You need stories to carry you through to the end. The stories that land deals are the ones that help the person who wants to buy your services to convince everyone else. When you provide your sponsor with the stories they need to land the deal, you'll win.

Next we'll find out what these land stories really are. We'll dissect them, with examples, to see how they work. Then, in the final chapter, I'll teach you how you can create and use your own. Are you ready to close more deals, bigger deals? Read on.

11. Your buyer on remote control

When your values are clear to you, making decisions is easy.

Roy Disney, Disney Corporation

You tell values stories to reduce your customer's fear of perceived risks. You tell sales teaching stories to help your future customer reach consensus in the decision committee in favour of your solution. The values story is the answer to the question, what happens if things go wrong after we decide? The teaching story is the answer to the problem of failing to decide, overcoming the 'do nothing' decision or the wrong decision. The values story provides comfort in the face of risk; the teaching story inspires action.

Let's look at each of the two Land stage story types in turn to understand exactly what they are.

Values stories and risk avoidance

Few significant purchases are made by a single person. Personally, Megan and I don't spend more than a couple of hundred dollars without consulting each other. Our family is a two-person decision team in all of our household expenditure decisions. For large B2B sales purchases you can count on many more decision makers. We involve other people in the decision process because we want to avert the risk of failure: it's a risk avoidance strategy and standard policy for most companies.

There are statistics about the average number of decision makers involved in a B2B sale. CEB reported an average of 5.4 decision makers in a 2014 study of more than 5000 stakeholders.[1] I don't know the relevance of those statistics for your business, but the rise of consensus-based decision making is real. In my experience there are between five and ten influencers, and sometimes more. Not all of those people are significant contributors to the decision, but they can veto it or throw obstacles in the path of a decision in your favour. You've used insight and success stories to locate and influence your sponsor, the person who wants your solution. But you also need to influence others on the decision committee. You may not be able to meet with them, but they are almost always concerned about risk. Your values stories will show these people that your company will overcome any problems that may potentially occur, or that those problems will never occur because of your company values.

Let's review some questions a buying committee might have before spending a few million dollars. Their first concern will be whether the decision will have a financial return. 'Will the supply company deliver what they say they'll deliver? Will we get the outcome we expect? What if there are problems and it doesn't go quite as planned? Will the supplier stand by us? What if there's a catastrophic failure? Will they still support us? What if there's a technical problem and the new system goes out of action for several days? Will they behave ethically in those situations? If we pay upfront, will we definitely still receive what we think we're purchasing? How can we be sure? If those things go wrong, then what? What would happen to our company? Could we continue to operate? Continue to trade? Will I lose my job? Will my team members lose their jobs?

People can build a mountain of negative hypotheticals about what could happen and expand those stories into deal-killing fantasies, if you're not careful. So what would really allay those fears?

One answer to a perceived risk is a success story, though you may not have other clients who have successfully navigated the particular risks of concern here. But a values story—a story about how your company behaves when things go wrong, for example—can be extremely powerful. It might seem counterintuitive to talk about things going wrong at this stage of a deal. In fact, your future client wants to hear this story. They're not convinced by the story that says everything will be perfect. That's not believable.

Several of my values story examples date from my time selling for the German multinational conglomerate Siemens. A core value of Siemens is 'reliable engineering that we stand behind'. I was struck by the number of stories on the theme of 'We stick with you until you get your outcome'. When I worked at Siemens in the mid 2000s it was still a company dominated by engineering, with hardly any 'sales culture', not an American-style marketing and sales–led company at all. But beneath the pragmatic, reserved engineering image were hundreds of values stories that influenced both clients and employees.

The train radio story

In May 2004 I experienced those values first-hand. I was working in Sydney on temporary transfer to help with the project management of a large tender. We had a team of fifty experts flown in from all parts of the world to assist, and the bid budget was $1.5 million. That large.

One Monday morning our state manager, John, arrived at work looking as if he hadn't slept. The previous day the radio network our company supplied to the metropolitan train operator had failed.[2] It was a network-wide failure, which meant no trains could run in Sydney that day. Fortunately it was a Sunday so it was much less disruptive than if it had been a weekday.

When John got the call about the failure, he abandoned his family plans and rushed to the customer's control room, where he worked alongside the customer's CEO scheduling buses to ensure minimum passenger disruption.

When the network was finally restored, John turned to the CEO and said, 'This is going to cost us, isn't it?'

The CEO's response was, 'Let's split the bus bill.'

What could have been an expensive, litigious conflict was resolved with a handshake in large part because John had shown empathy, accepted responsibility for the failure and given up his own time to help his customer in a crisis.

You can offer great service, but your service quality is only truly tested during the crisis of a service failure. The point of this story is to show that our employees stick by their customers whatever the situation, and they learn to do that through values stories. Delivery performance is what the client can count on; it's part of the company guarantee. We can, and do, write all sorts of guarantees into contracts but the stories, and the reputation that goes with them, are more reassuring than the contract. I'll return to values stories, with more examples, in the next chapter.

If you are wondering when your client sponsor should tell a values story, it is exactly at the point when people are saying (or thinking), 'What if it goes wrong? If we embark on this project and it doesn't work out, what's going to happen?' If your sponsor shares a relevant story at that point it will be highly persuasive. Here is an interesting thing, though. Your sponsor may not have the skill or inclination to tell your values story, but once you have shared the story, it will still work for you. Having heard the story, your sponsor will argue for your solution in a different way. They will be more committed to you. They will say something like, 'Look, I really trust these guys,' without knowing quite why, because the story had impact.

Values stories don't have to be about recovering from a service failure, but they need to demonstrate how your people work and behave under pressure. The hospitality industry is awash with these stories. There are hotel chains that regularly collect values stories. I call them 'lost wallet' stories, like when a hotel guest left their passport or wallet in the hotel and the hotel clerk saw it and drove across town or to the airport to return it without asking for anything in return. These stories highlight the values of honesty and service.

A lot of companies think they can just mandate corporate values through mission statements. That is completely misguided. The CEO or the leadership team think up some motherhood values statements and post them on the walls. Those don't persuade. They may even communicate the opposite sentiment if actions do not match the words. It's stories of people (especially leaders) who live the corporate values that are truly eloquent.

The HP Way

Hewlett-Packard (HP) is a storied company in the information technology sector. HP people were famous for their proactivity and accountability. Their code of conduct was called the 'HP Way'.[3] Their corporate tagline: 'We trust our people.'

The history of that tagline goes all the way back to the company's foundation in 1939, when it was a test equipment manufacturer. Every HP employee knows the story[4] of how co-founder Bill Hewlett came in to work on a weekend and found the equipment storeroom locked. He smashed the door to pieces with a fire axe and left a note on the smashed door, insisting it never be locked again *because HP trusts its people.*

A story that shows how a leader behaves is worth more than any number of corporate values statements. Employees and customers are influenced by what leaders do to demonstrate values much more than what they say or write. It's not an overstatement to say that story helped create one of the greatest companies of the 20th century, which in turn spawned the technology powerhouse of Silicon Valley. Steve Jobs got his first job at HP.

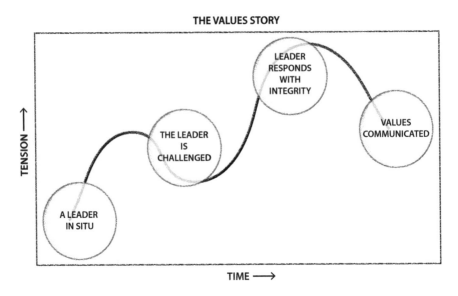

Figure 11.1: The Leader's Test—values story structure

Taglines and mission statements mean nothing. Pages of tender responses about your company values are worthless. A true story means everything. When a leader demonstrates the values of their company through storyable action—we call that *story triggering* —those values become part of company lore. When leaders by their actions demonstrate the company values, employees and customers follow.

When leaders by their actions demonstrate the company values, employees and customers follow.

Sales teaching stories

The second type of land story is the story that helps your future client through process aspects of the decision. This is the teaching story. What if the decision committee wastes time by worrying about things they need not worry about? What if there is an overbearing person on that committee who hogs the conversation and derails the process? How can I teach them to make the right decision?

Teaching stories are context specific. Typical obstacles that decision teams face when they have to make an important purchasing decision include issues such as lack of urgency, individuals delaying the process, inability to get agreement, standoffs within the committee due to personality conflict and turf battles over resource allocation. Each requires a targeted story.

The largest and most complex deals are normally closed by the most seasoned salespeople because they have the stories about how to close these types of deals. Often their skill is unconscious; they are unaware of the stories they have or how they use them. But when you know these stories exist you can seek them out and share them with your less experienced salespeople and your clients, particularly your sponsor, to help them resolve those closed-door internal decision issues.

The resident strong man

Before there was an iPod or iTunes[5], I pitched a music content platform to a large media company. It was a complex deal requiring the expertise of dozens of people from our company and a similar number from the customer. When we had locked down a viable solution and business model, it was time for the final price negotiation. Up to that point we'd worked with the customer team in a collaborative partnership.

That changed when the customer wheeled in their chief negotiator, a person we came to call the 'resident strong man' (we used a slightly different descriptor) because of his behaviour during the negotiations.

Picture the scene. All their many technical and business people down one side of a long table, a similar number of our experts down the other side, with negotiator at the head. As the negotiations commenced, strong man proceeded to pull apart the scope and business model. He demanded impossible quality levels and an unworkable business model. There were loud threats of legal action. We weren't being collaborative anymore—this was nasty. I was used to ambit claims, but these demands were outrageous.

I remember walking disconsolately back to our office and confiding with a more experienced colleague that I thought the deal could not be closed.

'Why not ring him up and request a private meeting?' my colleague asked.

'Really? I can do that?' I hadn't even thought of that possibility.

I rang strong man and arranged to meet him in his office, where we talked for two hours. I discovered he had a poor understanding of the project he was negotiating, a vulnerability I would never have guessed from his aggressive approach. So I shifted tactics and took the time to educate him. I explained why certain aspects of our tender were non-negotiable because they would compromise the outcome his company wanted to achieve.

It took several more full-scale meetings to close the sale, but the chief negotiator was no longer behaving badly, even though outwardly he was as tough as before. Subsequent meetings focused on the negotiable areas and we eventually struck a deal. Meeting the negotiator privately was the turning point. And finding a way to teach him how to close the deal without losing face in front of his team.

I've used that story to teach my salespeople how to 'unstick' negotiations and to help my customer sponsor do the same in their internal decision meetings (you can use this story too). It's critically important to allow people to keep face when they need to back down from an untenable position. For this, privacy is paramount.

Your teaching story needs to match the situation you're dealing with. It needs to convey the right emotion. In the resident strong man story, the chief negotiator was a bombastic person who had thrown himself into a situation he didn't understand without knowing how to back out of it. We needed to manage his potential embarrassment and loss of face.

Cost of delay

With an urgency problem, we need to create a sense of urgency and make people feel the loss they would experience if they missed the opportunity. People don't like to lose a negotiation, but they often don't appreciate what's at stake when they can't come to a decision. Fear of loss and urgency can be conveyed in a story. And the strange thing about urgency stories is they don't need to be about your specific business; you can generate the urgency emotion with an analogous story.

A real estate company I've been working with is operating in a hot market that is peaking. Prices are starting to fall, but prices have risen spectacularly over the past few years so the tendency for the seller is to hold out for an unrealistic price and fail to sell. That attitude could be expensive for the property seller, but it's a difficult situation for the real estate agent. The agent's opinion, assertions and advice will not be heard because of a perceived conflict of interest. What's needed is an urgency story. I told them the following story from my personal experience.

The pink house story

The suburb I live in has an unusually high level of house reconstruction because the land value is so high. In our street almost every house has been demolished and replaced with a modern house sporting a basement carpark, wine cellar, cinema and private lift. In 2014, two neighbouring, similar houses were sold and demolished to clear the way for construction of new houses. The average sale price was $4 million on an average lot size of 600 square metres.

The builder at property A used a construction method I've not seen before: modular formwork for the concrete walls that was quick to erect. The house flew out of the ground. It was finished to a high standard and sold nine months after demolition for $9 million in a hot market in 2015.

The builder at property B is still on the basement after three years of construction. Which is just great for the neighbours (not)!

Setting aside the aggravation for the neighbours, think about the financial cost of building a house that slowly. The time value of $4 million is $160,000 a year at current interest rates — that's what a mortgage would be costing. If it had been completed two years ago and rented, it could have returned $250,000 a year in the current stable rental market. But the biggest 'cost' is likely to be in the house value, if it is sold on completion. Property B could easily sell for less than property A because of a cooling market. A $2 million loss looks quite likely.

Owner B is likely to lose a minimum of $1,250,000, and probably much more, just because of the delay. People don't think carefully enough about the cost of time.

The key criterion of the teaching story is it must match the emotional situation. It doesn't have to be exactly the same situation, but it must deliver the emotional impact of that situation. It also must convey insights about human behaviour. The resident strong man story conveys insights about saving face; the pink house story conveys insights about the value of time, highlighting the cost of delay.

Most people don't think about the financial impact of choosing a slow builder. They're focused on who will deliver the best finished product or the lowest total cost. Choosing the slow builder adds significantly to the overall cost, and choosing a faster builder frees up more money to spend on fixtures and fittings. You can buy quite a lot with $1,250,000.

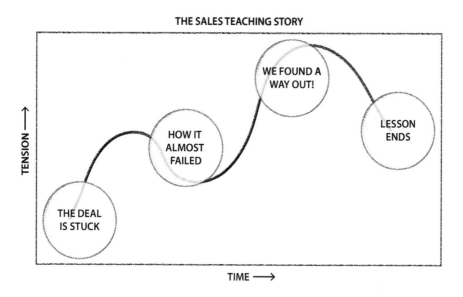

Figure 11.2: The Sales Teaching Story—a problem-solving journey

Keep connecting in the decision phase

Maybe you agree with me about hook stories that connect and fight stories that differentiate, but you don't agree with this landing the deal stuff. You may think, for example, that telling a story about how your company dealt with a screw-up is too risky. Even to hint that things could go wrong is unwise. Or you may think it's inappropriate to try to influence matters during the customer's decision phase. 'We should just let the client get on with the decision and not interfere.'

My experience is that if you don't exert any influence through the decision phase, you increase your client's chances of not getting their best result. My first story in the Land phase about failing to sell a telecommunications system (the Hell's Gateway story) is a prime example. The client did not choose the best solution and I could have helped prevent that poor outcome. If you're confident that your solution is best for your client, you should be confident to continue exerting influence all the way to contract signature. Otherwise you and your future customer will lose out.

> **If you're confident that your solution is best for your client then be confident to exert influence all the way to contract signature. Otherwise your client will lose out.**

Is there a risk of telling the wrong teaching story? Can we mess it up? It depends on how well connected you are with your sponsor, but teaching stories are low risk for a couple of reasons. The first is people often don't notice stories. When you tell a teaching story there's a reasonable chance that the message gets through to your sponsor's brain and they don't realise you're influencing them. That's the magic of stories. If your story misses the mark, then there is nothing lost; it's like you said nothing. The second reason its low risk is there's nothing malicious about your story.

Your intent is ethical. You're telling the story to help your client solve a problem. I put on my best sales manager voice and deliver the teaching. 'Your situation reminds me of when …' I'm teaching them how to sell. You'll be amazed at how well this works.

There's a saying the best sales managers know: 'You need to teach your client how to buy and you need to teach them how to sell.'[6] Teaching them how to buy means showing them why they should buy your products and services. Teaching them how to sell means showing them how to get the decision made in their organisation.

To summarise, the three critical activities to get you through this difficult period of landing the deal are:

1. Tell your values stories to help allay the perception of risk.

2. Use your sales management skills by telling sales teaching stories to smooth the decision process.

3. Reiterate your insight and success stories. 'Others have done it, and done it successfully. So it's not a big risk to change.'

These activities will guide the decision team through the process to make the right decision. We're talking here about landing the big deal, and big deals — even in big companies — happen rarely. When they do, we celebrate. Champagne bottles lined up, everyone's congratulating you. You're the hero. You made it happen. It wasn't obvious how you did it. Your stories worked invisibly and subtly in the background, so you're a magician! More importantly, you won a deal that your competitors might have won. You've taken business from them, and your client got the value of your products and services, a real solution to their problem. It's a tremendous win. Let's celebrate!

Now you understand exactly what values and teaching stories are. In the final chapter we learn how to prepare your own land stories.

12. Influence in the dark

Sometimes, if you want to change a man's mind, you have to change the mind of the man next to him first.

Megan Whalen Turner, *The King of Attolia*

After you've submitted your proposal, or your massive tender, your stories come out to play on their own, weaving their magic without you. You're not going to be in the decision meeting, so you're relying on your values stories and your sales teaching stories to get you to the contract signature. Landing the big fish.

In this chapter I'm going to show you exactly how to collect, construct and deliver values stories and sales teaching stories.

Collecting values stories

The first part of this process is to think carefully about the risks your future customers will face when they implement your solution. What would happen if it failed? How would your company respond in that situation? What exactly might fail? Can you think of stories that show that their outcome is guaranteed?

Your customer service and operations departments can be a good source of these stories, but your company isn't the ultimate source of stories about risk. People in your company don't think the way your buyer does. The best source for these stories is your existing clients, the people already using your solution. Why not have a conversation with them? Ask why they bought your products and services and what they were worried about at the time? What happened to those concerns? What was it that reassured them? From these conversations you can identify your top five buyer concerns. You'll also be able speak with other customers in their language, rather than using vendor-speak. They won't mind talking about this. If you're in a perceptive and curious frame of mind, listening carefully and prompting for more details, you can get some fascinating stories. You'll also get good feedback for your operations people about what your clients like and dislike about your service.

CarMax is the largest used car company in the United States.[1] Its entire business is structured to allay the buyer's fear of having to deal with a salesperson in a car yard. They have set up their company to avoid having salespeople put on the hard sell. Their marketing explains that everyone pays a fixed price and every car comes with a warranty.

CarMax is an example of a company that has built its business around understanding and allaying their buyer's fears. Values stories work in the same way. When you really understand your future customer's fears, then you can collect stories that showcase how you manage those situations. The values story says, 'Yes, it could happen. But here's what would happen if it does, and here's how we guarantee that you'll still be okay. You'll still get your outcome.'

In chapter 9, I mentioned the testimonial phone call as a method for getting success stories. The same process can be used to uncover values stories.

Armed with a list of my client's top five or ten good customers, I call each of them. After explaining why we're talking with our best clients, I ask them to tell me about their history with my client. 'How did you engage them? What made you notice them? Why did you decide to go with them?' These are positive questions. Then I ask, 'What did you fear might go wrong? What were the things that you were concerned about at the time? How did my client go about allaying those concerns?'

With this information from their current customers, I then interview my client's key operations staff, such as the head of customer service or of operations or the implementation. I'll say, 'Your clients have said they were worried about this and this. Could you tell me a story where that might have happened? Or when it looked like it was going to happen?' Then I ask, 'How did you make sure that risk didn't eventuate?'

That's how to get your values story topics.

Values stories are normally sourced from within our company, but the best story topics or situations come from current customers. You need to look in both places.

It's critically important that the leaders of your organisation are involved in collecting, endorsing and telling values stories. For example, if your client is concerned about whether you will provide good support and be there when they need you, 24/7, it won't help to tell a story of exemplary support if your company doesn't live up to that values promise.

If your positioning and client expectation is that you provide the lowest price, then your values stories will reflect relentless price cutting, because lowest price is your value. The company's values must be modelled and lived by its leaders. My story of the Siemens state manager spending his Sunday with his client when the train radio network failed is an example of a leader triggering a story about behaviour that his staff will notice and copy. When leaders model and trigger these stories, they travel like wildfire.

IKEA's humble leadership

When I moved with my family to Moscow in the year 2000, the Swedish furniture retail giant IKEA had just opened its first store in Russia. I remember the publicity CEO Ingvar Kamprad received when he helped out in the freight department on launch day. *Forbes* magazine reported[2] 'mystified Russian shoppers being chatted to by Kamprad in rudimentary to non-existent Russian. They'd ask the staff, "Who is that old man?" When we told them he was the CEO, the reaction was pure disbelief.'

The Hewlett-Packard fire axe story is similar. Hypothetical or theoretical values don't cut it. Your company values must be demonstrated through action. As sales leaders, you know better than most what your customers most value. You can influence your leaders to live the company values and model the behaviours that your customers need to see. Your staff and customers believe what leaders do, not what they say, and values stories are the emblems of what leaders do.

Collectively, we can engineer and trigger values stories by living the company values. That is the way to create values stories in your organisation. Most of the business textbooks on storytelling come out of the domains of change management and leadership. There is a growing realisation in the business world that leaders need to be storytellers. The best leaders (and salespeople) have always been storytellers, but now the techniques are becoming more recognised and better understood.

Story: a window to corporate values

When I joined Siemens in 2003, I needed to learn the culture of the company. I'd spend seventeen years in the oil and gas industry with Schlumberger. Siemens and Schlumberger are outwardly similar. Both are massive engineering technology companies (with revenues in 2016 of US$100 billion and US$30 billion respectively), but I soon learned that their corporate values are quite different. Schlumberger dominates its chosen markets with innovation leadership. Siemens also leads with innovation but its primary value is delivery promise.

I asked my new colleagues, 'Why do people buy from Siemens?' Our products didn't seem to be the best, they were often not the latest technology, or the sexiest, and our marketing was abysmal. Why is the company so successful? The answer was, 'Because it works! Siemens always delivers.' If you're spending tens or hundreds of millions of dollars and your new system doesn't work, you lose your job and maybe your business. Over and over I heard stories that backed up Siemens' delivery promise.

The subsea blunder

When I first joined Siemens, they were still talking about a contract that had gone wrong a few years before I joined. Siemens had successfully bid to supply and install a subsea telecommunications cable under several hundred kilometres of ocean across the Spencer Gulf in South Australia.

A wrong assumption was made (by the client) about the composition of the seabed. Limited testing indicated that the seabed was mostly mud when in fact it was rock. Millions of dollars of cost overrun trenching through rock was absorbed by Siemens. They lost money but delivered the project on time, because delivering the client's outcome is a key company value.

Disaster inverted

A few years later, in 2005, Siemens was in the news because of a high-profile mishap with a subsea electricity cable that now connects Tasmania to mainland Australia. Electricity would be transmitted under 400 kilometres of sea with direct current, connecting the electricity grids of Tasmania and Victoria—a huge boost in electricity security for both states. Siemens was contracted to supply the inverter transformer components that convert direct electrical current to alternating current, and vice versa.

The ship transporting the massive inverters from Germany to Australia lost its rudder in big seas in the Great Australian Bight. All six inverter transformers were damaged beyond repair.

The publicity-shy engineering company found itself front-page news because a critical piece of public infrastructure was at risk of serious delay. I remember discussing the fallout with country CEO, Albert Goller at the time. When there are difficulties with large projects like this, often the various parties take a self-protecting legal position. The Siemens world board took the decision to fast-track the manufacture of new transformers regardless of legal claims pending.[3]

Normal lead-time to construct the inverters was more than 12 months. Siemens had them rebuilt and commissioned in record time and hit the delivery time.

This type of story has impact. Imagine your client sponsor in a closed-door decision meeting and a stakeholder asks, 'What if they don't deliver?' or 'Will it definitely work?' Your sponsor says, 'But it's Siemens!' Your sponsor is convinced the project will be delivered successfully and their tone of voice carries that conviction to the decision committee. Why are they convinced? Because they've heard your values story.

How did I construct that values story? Let's break it down. I've told the story many times. Probably a different way each time, but in telling it often you learn the bits you need. For that reason, one or two high-impact values stories are more powerful than many average stories. I needed to paint word pictures of the main events. Remember, a story is a sequence of events. I started the story with a time marker and a place marker. Then I told you what was at stake. Then I took you on a journey through the things that went wrong (the rudder failing, the inverters being smashed). You couldn't predict what would happen next. Then I resolved the story by describing the company's actions and made the business point about values. Which was: *Siemens always delivers*.

Your first-pass story is always too long. Until you've practised, it will contain too much detail. You can't take all the detail out. For example, the image of the ship plunging through huge seas is an important part of the story. If you remove important detail, your account becomes a bland commentary rather than a story.

So there is a balance. Choose your event marker first. Set up the starting event, one or two complication events, a turning point and a resolution. Then describe each event in sequence.

When you finish the story, it's better to let your listener draw their own conclusion about the point of the story, and it's definitely better not to mention the word 'story'. Preface the story with why you are telling it: 'This reminds me of another situation when delivery was critical …' If the story doesn't make your point, it's not a great story. While the narrative needs to make your point, your listener fills in the details of the story in their own mind. If you tell them too much, they can't create it themselves. You've got to give them the framework but let them complete the story themselves and expand their own mental model. Then they really get it and they'll remember it.

You tell your values story to your client sponsor. Should you ask your sponsor explicitly to pass on the story to other decision makers? If possible, yes. I ask my sponsor to tell me about the people involved in the decision and what their likely concerns are. Then I can tell a story to the sponsor that addresses their key concern. I might suggest my sponsor retell the story but I can't take that for granted, or expect the sponsor to do a great job without story training. But whether they do or not, when objections crop up that could be answered by the values story your sponsor will be decisive and persuasive, because they've assimilated the story.

That's much better than someone raising a potential issue in a decision meeting and your sponsor responding with a weak 'I have no idea about that. Yeah, that could be a problem'. And before you know it the entire decision committee is dwelling on unlikely negative consequences.

You'll have noticed that good communication with your sponsor throughout the Land stage is imperative. That's the result of all your good story work in the Hook and Fight stages. There is an interesting counter-situation that sometimes occurs. That's when you need to tell the client's story back in your own organisation to get the deal across the line. In sales we sit in the middle as the link between our company and our future customer. The larger and more complex the deal, the more likely that both sides will have to compromise, and you often have to use your influence skills on your own management.

This might sound strange, but I'll tell you a story.

The safety fraud story

When I was working in the facility services business in 2012, we were in the final throes of a large tender (how we manoeuvred our way onto the tender list is another teaching story). The tender was for catering and cleaning services for a large mining area in Australia. The significant issue for the client was safety at the mine site. There were tens of thousands of workers at these mining areas, and somewhere between 10 percent and 15 percent of them were support people who did the cooking, cleaning and maintenance.

Many of those services staff were casual labourers and their retention rate was low, but they were doing potentially dangerous work and their injury rate was high. Perversely, the people doing the mining work, operating massive equipment, were well trained in safe work practices and had low injury rates. Reducing injury rates for the support staff was a key concern for my sponsor (we'll call him Derek). Derek's idea was to ensure the winning supplier's contract put significant profit at risk in the case of accidents.

I had made an excellent connection with Derek and we were at the point of making a best and final price proposal. Derek and I spoke on the phone late one evening and I raised my concern that we had not put enough profit at risk in our offer. Derek agreed, saying, 'It's almost like you haven't listened to us.' I explained that I could not cut the price further, as we were at our limit. Derek had a suggestion: 'How about increasing your overall price so you can put more profit at risk?'

That's the first and only time I've had a client suggest we raise our price. Since my conversation was privileged, it was my job to persuade my company to do something they had never done: increase the final price offer. I needed to persuade my management team without letting on how I knew the price rise would work.

I told the true story about how the client management team before Derek had lost their annual bonuses and been demoted because one of the facility companies had colluded with the mining company to hide accidents. That incident forced a company-wide change to the way contracts were written with respect to safety. I used that story to highlight my client's critical value, which was safety.

Through the customer's values story, I got the price rise and we put more profit at risk. We won the deal. That $35 million a year deal is still running. To date it's been worth more than $150 million.

In this case, I told the story internally to influence my company. It could also be a sales teaching story. It quite often happens that to close a complex deal you need to influence your own company. Once again you see how critical it is to have first 'hooked' your sponsor using connection stories.

VALUES STORY—STEPS AND QUESTIONS
What are the essential values of your company?
Which job roles most need to exemplify those values?
Interview people in those roles and ask for stories.
Who was the character in the story?
What did they do that was special?
What was the setting and setup for the story?
How did others react?
Interview the most senior leader you have access to.
How does that leader demonstrate the key values?
Can you or your leaders trigger a values story?

Figure 12.1: Values story cheat sheet

Teaching stories: learning from another's experience

Let's have a closer look at the sales process teaching stories. I tell these stories as if my sponsor was one of my direct report sales-people. I've been a sales manager for many years and I know that if I tell my sales guys an appropriate story, they can work out their problems themselves. If they come to me with an issue, I don't tell them do this or do that. I'll say, 'Reminds me of another time when this happened …' In the same way, if you tell your sponsor a sales process story, they learn from your experience. There isn't any other way they can learn, by the way! You only learn from experience — your own or someone else's.

There will be people in your company who have guided customers through the decision-making process up to contract signing. They'll have a mental checklist of things that can go wrong. We have a good memory for painful events. Find those people, the experienced dealmakers in your organisation, and ask them, 'What tends to go wrong? What did you have to do? Tell me more about a time when the deal went wrong.' With these stories you can arm your sponsor with deal-closing tactics.

If you're selling new products and services that no one has ever sold before, you may need to seek out stories from adjacent businesses. However, many teaching stories, such as the resident strong man negotiating story, are applicable across most business situations.

There are two deal situations that are so common that you should have teaching stories prepared for them. These are:

- Gaining internal agreement

- Urgency or cost-of-delay story.

Can it go wrong?

A potential issue with 'sales teaching stories' is choosing the wrong story. For example, while negotiating with the 'resident strong man', I received advice from one other person. The advice was to walk away from the negotiation. 'Show them you mean business and walk away.' I'm certain that advice would have been fatal for the deal. The negotiator would have marched our competitor in and done the deal with them.

No doubt there are stories of walking away from a negotiation that turned out well, with a deal still being made. My experience is that in complex B2B negotiations walking away is an extreme move that almost always leads to the deal collapsing. Walking away doesn't set a good precedent for a future working relationship. You must select your story with care. Stories are highly memorable persuasion tools for specific incidents. If you choose the wrong incident, you shoot yourself in the foot.

Having access to people with experience during deal making is important. That's the reason why the bigger the deal, the more experienced the dealmakers are. It's much harder to get big deals done if you haven't had experience of what can go wrong. Having access to your sponsor through the decision process is the second important key.

Certain deal closing situations are common and predictable. Lack of urgency and failure to get agreement are routine problems, so it makes sense to have prepared 'generic' stories about these situations. Remember, your teaching stories don't need to be about the same client situation, but they do need to evoke the same emotion and action. Ask yourself, how do you want your sponsor to feel and how should they act?

In a situation like the resident strong man story, I want my sponsor to feel diplomatic and conciliatory and to be prepared to negotiate one-on-one behind the scenes. In the case of lack of urgency, I want my sponsor to be wary of lost opportunity and act by making a decision to close the deal. A good connection with your sponsor is your insurance policy. If you're trying to guess from outside the decision-making circle, if you don't have a good connection with your sponsor, then you risk telling the wrong story.

Suppose you're stuck. The decision-making committee seem to be taking forever. You need an urgency story. Seek out one of your experienced guys, explain the situation and ask for advice. As you listen, look out for and prompt for a suitable story: 'In your case, what was at stake? What did your client miss out on? What did that cost them? What were the consequences?' Then you need framework details so you can structure your story: 'When and where did that happen? Tell me about [the main character]? How did [main character] feel through the process? How did it end up?'

You may think it's too late to develop a new story when a deal is stalled. It's not too late because big deals take weeks or months to wrap up. So you have time to find a good story. It is too late to change the values of your company, but it's not too late to find a good values story based on existing values and behaviours.

The formula for constructing teaching stories is the same as that for other basic stories. You need to frame the situation in a setting. Where and when did it happen? Explain what's at risk, what are the stakes. Who is the character in your story? Then take your listener on the journey of complications to a resolution that teaches the point you want to make.

In the pink house cost-of-delay story, I used contrast to show the difference between acting now and delaying. Consider situation A versus situation B. In this structure you sketch out each scenario, explain why delay may look okay on the surface but why acting now is better. In Australia, a retirement pension company uses TV and print advertisements under the banner 'Compare the pair'.[4] The ad compares the financial situation of two people, one who delays investing in her retirement fund and another who invests in the advertiser's product. It's a simple, effective visual.

Emotional content is critical when it comes to telling a cost-of-delay story. Choose your emotion words carefully and they'll feel it. Dwell on the loss and embarrassment and your listener will experience those emotions at a subconscious level. Acting on your solution now is the instant antidote to that feeling of loss.

It's unlikely your sponsor will tell your cost-of-delay story in a decision meeting, but having heard the story their commitment to urgency will be more robust. Their tone of voice and body language will be more confident. If it's a really good story, your sponsor may tell it, but the story has power even if it's not retold.

TEACHING STORY—STEPS AND QUESTIONS
Make a list of your most common deal sticking points.
Seek out experienced closers.
Collect examples of analogous situations.
What was the setting? When and where?
Describe the situation.
What was at stake, in business and personal terms?
How was the problem resolved?
What was the consequence? (Be specific.)
What is the story message?
Give each story a memorable name.

Figure 12.2: Sales teaching story cheat sheet

Build a story library

Just as with hook and fight stories, it's important to collect and refine your land stories. Most of the sales teams I've worked with have high staff churn rates compared with other departments. A staff turnover of between 20 and 30 percent in a year is common in high-pressure teams. The sales role isn't for everyone and sales leaders lose salespeople all the time. How do I get my stories to the new sales guys if I don't have a system for storing them? This is so important, yet few companies seem to have a system for capturing stories. If you don't capture your stories in a story library you'll lose them, and when you lose good stories you lose competitive advantage. Your company becomes weaker. Your job as a sales leader is to get the team performing better. You should be asking yourself, 'How do I create a team of storytellers?' The answer starts with recording your company stories and making them available to the team. That's a concrete system for improving sales in your company.

Landing the deal checklist

✓ Does your company operate under guiding values that benefit your customer? Find a story that exemplifies those values.

✓ Are there common, predictable ways that potential clients fail to secure your products and services? Find teaching stories that will reassure them and decide in their best interests.

✓ Upload your company values and teaching stories to your story library so everyone in the team can access the stories.

Conclusion

We write to taste life twice, in the moment and in retrospect.

Anaïs Nin, French-born American author

I challenged you at the beginning of the book, in my author's note, to imagine you had just eight months to sell $20 million of products and services in an industry you didn't know. Now you have the story tools, please permit me to share one last story.

Original insight

When I joined the facility services industry in 2012, I was immediately thrown in the deep end responding to tender requests. I became aware that almost every facility services contract in the Australian resources industry had a requirement for local Aboriginal participation in the workforce, such as 5, 10 or 20 percent of the workforce.

The requirement made sense. Mining companies operating under licence on Indigenous lands should employ local Indigenous people as part of their contribution to the local community. But I noticed that my company was not compliant. We did not meet the required participation rates, and the targets were not enforced.

I was curious about that.

I wondered whether the mining companies were just ticking the box to show they were trying to employ Indigenous Australians. But when I talked to the mining executives, I found that, no, they viewed it as a very important requirement. They were exasperated that their contractors could not comply, but it was a mystery to them how to achieve those targets. The failure rates were high.

Then I became aware that one of our contracts in the far north-west of Australia, in an area known as the Kimberley, had more than 40 percent Indigenous participation at a site with a hundred of our facility support staff. How could that be when our other sites, and competitor sites, struggled to achieve 5 percent?

As the business developer, I decided to investigate. I didn't get a satisfactory answer from the people I spoke with at head office so I flew to the Argyle Diamond Mine. It's the world's primary producer of rare pink diamonds. I was introduced to the contract manager, John Mustey, and we talked about the challenges of Indigenous employment. (I also talked with the Indigenous and non-Indigenous camp staff.)

As I listened to John, the enormity of the problem became apparent. Also becoming apparent was the solution!

John talked about how difficult it was to hire Indigenous people. The HR policies of big mining companies, and my company, wouldn't let you hire anyone with a criminal record, but a disproportionate number of Indigenous Australians have criminal records (as is, sadly, often the case worldwide with indigenous peoples). New employees had to provide identity documents such as a driver's licence and birth certificate, but many had lost those documents. They often didn't live in permanent housing so weren't able to maintain records. John's solution was to meet with the head of security at the mining company and argue for them. He'd say, 'I'll be responsible for these people. Let them into the camp and I'll look after them. They'll be okay.' He'd vouch for them.

The next issue was that many Indigenous people had never held down a job of any kind. John's approach was to split every job into micro tasks and teach each task in turn. If they've never made a bed before, they're going to spend a week or two just making beds. John split up his roster so he could split the tasks. Step by step, Indigenous workers learned how to do a complete job, then how to do a different job. So they rotated around all the jobs in the camp and became useful regular employees.

Indigenous people often have large, close-knit family groups. If there's a death, and deaths are common in rural Aboriginal communities, it's expected that everyone in their family or kinship group attend the funeral. And those funerals can last a week or much longer, so camp staff would often go to a funeral and never come back.

Anyone leaving the mine site had to get John's permission and he'd check whether they really had to go. If John sensed they didn't want to go, he'd refuse permission and see the relief in their eyes. If they did need to go, John would ask, 'How long do you need to be gone for?' If they said, 'Two days,' John would say, 'Okay, I'll have a car and driver waiting for you. They'll bring you back to camp after two days.' John knew from experience that once they went to the funeral, if he didn't bring them back, he may not get them back.

As I listened to these stories I understood how John had achieved such high participation rates at his site. His patience, compassion, understanding and willingness to work around the rules were the keys to this success. Having people in charge like John made it possible. I realised that in most camps neither the mining company staff nor the facility services contractors were committed to Indigenous participation, and there were many easy ways to reject them.

But when people like John flip that around and ask, 'What does it take to employ these people?' A different picture emerges. Argyle diamond mine was a fascinating site to tour. I saw Indigenous and non-Indigenous staff sitting together at meal times. Laughing and enjoying each other's company. Friends. All part of the same team, doing the same job. Problem solved. What an amazing insight!

This is an insight story for our times. Seeing how John and his crew solved that problem made me want to be part of the solution for a disadvantaged group in our society, and it changed my mind to identify with the plight of Indigenous people in my country.

I've told that story as an insight story, with me as the 'researcher'. That's how I told it to help change attitudes and win business at other sites. It could also be told as a success story for the mining company, as a key staff story about John Mustey or as a values story to motivate the rest of my company. There are multiple stories, depending on who you cast as the main character. Your task is to open your mind and seek out stories.

Within this story are elements for success in any sales challenge you set yourself. Your curiosity and drive to uncover the seven stories is the secret to solving any sales challenge that you undertake.

I'd like to offer a multi-choice benefit question. Would you like:

- ☐ more profit?
- ☐ better client outcomes?
- ☐ better relationships?
- ☐ more responsibility?
- ☐ bigger deals?
- ☐ more fun?
- ☐ an easier life?

Tick as many boxes as you like. It's your choice. All these options are open to you with seven stories storytelling.

A couple of pitfalls to watch out for. Don't be a story bore. Or, as my writing 'Sherpa' Kath Walters would say, a 'story bully', using stories to bludgeon your audience insensible. You can get carried away with stories and talk for too long. Sales is a contact sport, and our artistry reaches its pinnacle with the story *exchange*. If you fill the conversation with your own stories, there's no space for your client's story. That's the real secret. Allow space to share and then create a new story with your future customer. That's what the story exchange sets up.

And here's a cautionary tale. You've learned about a powerful persuasion tool, but all tools can be used for good or for ill. The *intent* behind your storytelling is crucial. You must use stories with the intention of getting the best outcome for your client. When you use a persuasion tool only for selfish ends, you run a serious risk. You may achieve short-term success, but you risk being found out and debarred from future business, excluded from the business high table. There's no personal growth down that path. Use your stories with the intention of getting the best outcome for your client, and only then for yourself. Believe me, if your intentions are honourable you will reap the full rewards of your sales skills.

Use your stories with the intention of getting the best outcome for your client, and only then for yourself.

'The eyes are the windows to your soul,' according to an ancient saying. Reflecting on my career, I've found that stories are windows to the soul. When you listen to another's story carefully, with an open heart, the truth of their character shines through. A couple of times in my career I've missed the warning signs of troubled souls and ended up working for or with someone on the sociopathic spectrum. You can avoid significant pain by listening carefully to other people's stories. You can also find great joy and connection. Use stories to navigate your way through life, to gauge who you want to work with and the kinds of business relationships you want. You'll get to the best and safest destinations by asking others for their story.

The purpose of this book is to reveal a hidden ingredient to sales success. It's a distillation of all I've learned in more than twenty years of selling and leading sales teams. Blend storytelling with your favourite sales process and you'll be on your way to a gourmet meal. It won't replace everything else you've learned, but storytelling will provide the catch of the day—the centrepiece to transform a bland meal to something memorable and unforgettable.

Good storytelling needs practice. This is not a get-rich-quick scheme. I've given you the framework. It's not complicated, but it requires (pleasurable) effort. Go out, collect stories, notice them, refine them, practise and then tell them! That is my final exhortation. What's the point of having a magic potion and not using it? Go to it, or risk slipping back into the jargon-laden world of bland opinion, bullet points and assertions.

Tell your stories.

I've written this book with sales leaders in mind. When you take on the challenge of managing a sales team you are confronted with a long list of possible management interventions, many fraught with risk. Should you install a CRM? Rebalance territories? Implement a training program? Increase or decrease your sales team? Tinker with the commission scheme (heaven forbid!)? So many options. I believe creating a team of storytellers and building a story library should be high on your list. Stories are rocket fuel for sales teams. They motivate, energise, create connection and close deals.

Note the effect each of your stories has and seek out the best ones. A few, high-quality stories are better than any number of bland anecdotes. Collect the best stories and treasure them. Then go out and share them.

Thank you for reading my book. I wish for you a storied business life.

Acknowledgements

I'm not a good advice-taker but I'm so grateful for the professionals on this project: Kath Walters, displaced from a career in journalism and now creating new authors. Jem Bates, the master editor, I'm in awe! And Michael Hanrahan the publishing project manager, thank you.

As a group, we salespeople have many fine qualities but attention to detail is not foremost in our skillset. So finding salespeople to carefully review the book was problematic. Geoffrey Dirago and David Black rose brilliantly to the task. I thank you both for your thoroughness and insightful contributions! I also had late entries to the volunteer reviewer ranks and acknowledge the detailed contributions of Diane Hewat and Tony Hughes. Vladimir Roytblat, Frank Palinkas, Steve Tot, Robin Moustaka, Nigel Hart and Sue Findlay also read the manuscript and gave plenty of encouragement and feedback.

It turns out my memory is pretty good for stories but by no means infallible. To my story checkers, providers, participants and heroes: Alan Singer, Albert Goller, Andrew Wildy, Anthony Lonergan, Ben Zoldan, Brett Adamson, Chad Gates, Dan Drum, David Huck, Frank Palinkas, Franz Deimbacher, Jaime Phillips, Joe Losinno, John Mustey, John Chapman, Mariam Issa, Mark Elliot, Martyn Beardsell, Matt Lamont, Matt Nichols, Michael Givoni, Mike Bosworth, Nick Horton, Nigel Hart, Paul Ostergaard, Paul Thompson, Samantha Hanley, Stephen Denning, Steve Tot, Sue Findlay, Tabatha Cole, Voon Tat Choong and Wayne Meecham. My heartfelt thanks and I hope I haven't blown your cover …

You need all the information and support you can get when you embark on your first book and I would like to acknowledge and thank the published authors and marketing professionals who freely gave time to me: Liz Adams, Mike Bosworth, Shawn Callahan, Gabrielle Dolan, Graham Hawkins, Tony Hughes, David Masover, Cian Mcloughlin, Yamini Naidu and John Smibert.

Acknowledgements

I have so much to be grateful for at home. Starting with my parents, Lee and Ron, who brought me up as a curious adventurer. The best start possible. And home life with Megan and our boys, Cameron, Isaac and Nic. We've dragged them all over the world and they've turned out okay! They're a joy to be with, no parent could ask for more. While I was off filling up passports trying to be a salesperson, Megan was making our home in foreign countries and protecting the family. The rock of our family. All my love.

Appendices

Appendix A: Summary of the seven stories

Here's a summary of the seven stories with sample stories from the book to help you remember them.

HOOK — Stories to connect
1. Your personal story
   - Sue's story
2. Key staff story
   - Voon Tat story
3. Company creation story
   - Schlumberger in Russia

FIGHT — Stories to differentiate
4. Insight stories
   - The stomach ache story
5. Success stories
   - The financial wizard

LAND — Stories to close the deal
6. Values stories
   - The HP Way
7. Teaching stories
   - The resident strong man

Appendix B: Reference table for the seven stories

STORY TYPE	HERO	FRAME WORK	MESSAGE	PURPOSE	SAMPLE TONE
HOOK					
Personal	You	Simple	Why you do what you do. You are an authority. You can help.	Connect you with your future client by exchanging stories — so you can co-create the best outcome for each other	Humble
Key staff	Key staff	Simple	Why they do what they do. They can really help you.	Position key staff members for future acceptance, receive in turn their key staff stories and make a wider connection	Exalted, pumped up
Company	Founder(s) of the company	Simple	Why this company exists. What the company can do for you.	Make them a fan of your company and co-creator of its future	Trial by fire, service
FIGHT					
Insight	Researcher	Simple	How the insight was discovered	Allow your client to experience something they do not know about their own business but need to know	Serendipitous, curious, surprise
Success	Client	Hero's journey	How our client succeeded	Allow your client to experience the journey before they make the decision	Trial by fire, success
LAND					
Values	Company leader	Simple	What we care about as a company. How we reduce your risk.	Help your client understand how your company will behave in extreme circumstances	Wonder, surprise
Teaching	Sales expert	Simple	Practical advice, how to sell	Coach your sponsor(s) to navigate their internal political environment and make a decision	Teaching

Appendix C: Story catalogue

NAME	STORY TYPE	ABOUT	PAGE
Foreword by Mike Bosworth	Personal	Mike Bosworth's career in sales	ix
Materials manager story	Success	Bosworth's success story for new clients	xii
Fish in the swimming pool	Teaching	Why the fish metaphor	xvii
Six blind men	Teaching/Fable	Different perspectives	2
The mobiliser	Personal/Success	Mike's first big sale	4
The Prague Play	Teaching	Acting out a software demonstration	11
Matt and Joe's stories	Teaching	Natural storytellers	15
Artificial Intelligence	Teaching	AI for rock classification in the 1990s	17
The mobile tower story	Teaching	Pushback in conversations	24
The Zambia story	Insight/Teaching	Stephen Denning's World Bank change story	25
Golfing with Frank	Teaching	Importance of stories for memory	37
Skinning cats	Teaching	What a success story isn't	38
Getting the essence of the story	Personal/ Teaching	Interviewing skills	45
Teaching swimming story	Success/ Teaching	Emotion in story	48
World's shortest story	Teaching	Hemingway's story to win a bet	50
It's not just what you say …	Teaching	Storytelling voice tone	52
The mine safety story	Teaching	Sharing personal stories	63
David's tender story	Teaching	Importance of connection	64
The reluctant salesperson	Success/ Teaching	Using story to win new business	65
The Voon Tat story	Key Staff/ Teaching	Importance of key staff stories	66
The Schlumberger Russia story	Company	History of Schlumberger in Russia	69

NAME	STORY TYPE	ABOUT	PAGE
The sales trainer's nightmare	Teaching	Using story to break the ice	77
Mike's story	Personal	Mike's career story	80
Tabatha's story	Personal/ Teaching	Interviewing to get Tabatha's story	90
Sue's story	Personal	Sue's career story	92
Death by story	Teaching	Overusing story sharing	94
An oversharing story	Teaching	Limitations of story	95
The international expert	Key Staff/ Teaching	Alan and his technical salesperson storytelling	101
Inspiration downunder	Company	Downunder GeoSolutions company story	104
Five minutes to disaster	Company	First5minutes company story	107
Hiring salespeople	Insight	Hiring salespeople insight	117
Belief brainwaves	Teaching	Difficulty changing beliefs	119
Public Private Insight	Insight/Teaching	Developing a new business model with insight	122
The stomach ache story	Insight	Nobel Prize winning medical insight	129
Colourful insight	Insight	Xerox example from Challenger Customer	136
Einstein sees the light	Insight	Insight example from science	138
The financial wizard	Success	Financial services company cracks selling	146
Network scheming	Insight/Teaching	Finding a new solution in a sea of competition	156
Cialdini and the commitment experiment	Teaching	Persuasive principle of commitment	162
Hell's Gateway	Teaching	A sales failure story	169
The art exhibition ploy	Teaching	Influencing after tender submission	176
The train radio story	Values	A service recovery story	183
The HP Way	Values	Values triggered by the leaders actions	185
The resident strong man	Teaching	Saving face in a negotiation impasse	187
The pink house story	Teaching	Cost of delay story	190

NAME	STORY TYPE	ABOUT	PAGE
IKEA's humble leadership	Values	Values triggered by the leaders actions	198
The subsea blunder	Values	Demonstrating the company's values	199
Disaster inverted	Values	Demonstrating the company's values	200
The safety fraud story	Values/Teaching	Pitching the clients values internally	202
Original insight	Insight/Teaching	Indigenous hiring compliance	211

Appendix D: The story template

Story builder template

6 | **Story name** — (Make it memorable)

1 | **Point of the story?**

2 | **Setting (time and place)**

4 | **Key events and complications**

5 | **Turning point**

3 | **Resolution**

Hero of the story is?

Numbers = suggested construction order

Recommended reading

For students of sales, storytelling and psychology, here's a list of books that have influenced the structure and content of this book and influenced me over my sales career.

B2B Selling – Classic textbooks

The Challenger Customer: Selling to the Hidden Influencer Who Can Multiply Your Sales Results (2015) Adamson, Dixon, Spenner and Toman, Penguin Books

The Challenger Sale: Taking Control of the Customer Conversation (2011), Matt Dixon and Brett Adamson, Penguin Group

New Sales Simplified: The essential Handbook for prospecting and new business development (2013), Mike Weinberg, Amacom

The Secrets of Question-Based Selling: How the Most Powerful Tool in Business Can Double Your Sales Results (2000), Thomas Freese, Sourcebooks

Solution Selling: Creating Buyers in Difficult Selling Markets (1995), Michael T. Bosworth, McGraw Hill

SPIN Selling: The best validated sales method available today. Developed from research studies of 35,000 sales calls. (1988), Neil Rackham, McGraw Hill

Storytelling

Putting Stories to Work: Mastering Business Storytelling (2016)
Shawn Callahan, Pepperberg Press.

Tell to Win: Connect, Persuade, and Triumph with the Hidden Power of Story (2011), Peter Gruber, Crown Business

What Great Salespeople Do: The Science of Selling Through Emotional Connection and the Power of Story (2012), Michael Bosworth and Ben Zoldan, McGraw-Hill.

Business development

Crossing the Chasm, Edition: Marketing and Selling Disruptive Products to Mainstream Customers (1991), Geoffrey A. Moore, Harper Business

Brain science and psychology

The Elephant in the Brain: Hidden Motives in Everyday Life (2018), Kevin Simler and Robin Hanson, Oxford University Press

How Emotions Are Made: The Secret Life of the Brain (2017), Lisa Feldman Barrett, Houghton Mifflen and Harcourt

Influence: The Psychology of Persuasion (1984), Robert. B. Cialdini, Quill

On Intelligence (2004), Jeff Hawkins with Sandra Blakeslee, Times Books

Chapter notes

Introduction

1. Matt Dixon and Brett Adamson (2011), *The Challenger Sale: Taking Control of the Customer Conversation*, Mobiliser is a CEB/Challenger Sale buying persona or archetype.

Chapter 1: Why use stories?

1. I use 'cortex' and 'neocortex' interchangeably to mean the outer layer of the brain, the cerebral cortex. The word *cortex* comes from Latin, meaning bark, as in the bark of a tree. In biology it's used as a term for an outer layer. If you unfolded the human neocortex it would be about the size of a dinner napkin and about 2.5 mm thick.

2. Numenta (https://numenta.com), founded by Jeff Hawkins in 2005, is a private computer science and neuroscience research centre with the goal of reverse engineering the human neocortex.

3. The triune brain model seeks to understand the brain as three evolutionary separate parts: the reptilian brain, the 'emotional' limbic brain and the mammalian 'rational' brain. This model is no longer espoused by most comparative neuroscientists. See https://en.wikipedia.org/wiki/Triune_brain.

4. Lisa Feldman Barrett (2017), *How Emotions Are Made*, Houghton Mifflin Harcourt. I highly recommend this book if you are interested in the most recent understanding of how our brains work and how emotions are created.

5. Paraphrased from Andy Clark (2016), *Surfing Uncertainty: Prediction, Action and the Embodied Mind*. Oxford University Press.

6. Stephen Denning (2001), *The Springboard: How Storytelling Ignites Action in Knowledge-Era Organizations*, Butterworth Heinemann.

7. Patrick D. Nunn & Nicholas J. Reid (2016), Aboriginal Memories of Inundation of the Australian Coast Dating from More than 7000 Years Ago, *Australian Geographer*, vol. 47, issue 1.

8. Kevin Simler and Robin Hanson (2018), *The Elephant in the Brain: Hidden motives in everyday life*, Oxford University Press.

9. *Seinfeld* (TV series) (1995), 'The Beard', dialogue with George Costanza.

10. Shawn Callahan (2016), *Putting Stories to Work: Mastering Business Storytelling*, Pepperberg Press.

11. See www.anecdote.com, a great website for students of storytelling. You'll find excellent resources including a story library and a quiz to help you identify oral stories.

12. Solution Selling is a sales process that developed from Mike Bosworth's book *Solution Selling* (1995, McGraw-Hill). Solution Selling programs are delivered today by various licensed providers. SPIN Selling was a process developed from Neil Rackham's book *SPIN Selling* (1988, McGraw-Hill) and provided as training courses from Huthwaite Corporation, now part of the Miller Heiman group. Challenger Selling is a program provided by CEB/Gartner based on two books, *The Challenger Sale* (2011) and *The Challenger Customer: Selling to the Hidden Influencer Who Can Multiply Your Results* (2015) by Adamson, Dixon, Spenner and Toman.

Chapter 2: What is a story exactly?

1. Shawn Callahan (2016), *Putting Stories to Work: Mastering Business Storytelling*, Pepperberg Press. This book focuses on the practice of business storytelling, primarily for leadership and change management, and is highly recommended for salespeople.

2. The expression 'neurons that fire together, wire together' loosely describes the process of Hebbian learning; see https://en.wikipedia.org/wiki/Hebbian_theory.

3. There are multiple references to hierarchies in various cortical regions, particularly the primary sensory regions, for example in the visual cortex where cortical regions progressively process edges, then shape objects such as faces.

4. The best layperson's description of how sequence pattern memory and prediction works is found in Jeff Hawkins and Sandra Blakeslee (2004), *On Intelligence*, Times Books. It has been expanded and elaborated since 2004, but the basic hypothesis of sequence memory prediction still holds. A serious student may wish to dip into more recent articles such as Hawkins and Ahmad (2016), 'Why Neurons Have Thousands of Synapses, a Theory of Sequence Memory in Neocortex'. Professor Lisa Feldman Barrett's *How Emotions Are Made* (2017) is also an accessible read on memory prediction particularly as it relates to emotions in the neocortex.

5. Called the social competition hypothesis. See Rachael Rettner (July 2009), 'Why Are Human Brains So Big?', for a good discussion of the competing hypotheses. www.livescience.com/5540-human-brains-big.html.

Chapter 3: Tell me how it's done

1. *How Emotions Are Made* (2017), Lisa Feldman Barret, introduction and chapter 1 'the search for emotional fingerprints'.
2. A great book on empathy is *Against Empathy* (2016), by Paul Bloom, HarperCollins. Don't be put off by the title.
3. Michael Bosworth and Ben Zoldan (2012), *What Great Salespeople Do*, McGraw-Hill. One of the few books on storytelling dedicated to B2B sales. Highly recommended.
4. WhatsApp is a smartphone application owned by Facebook and available for Apple iOS and Google Android operating systems.
5. See *Persuasive Voice Tone* online training, master.mysevenstories.com/courses/persuasive-voice-tone.

Chapter 4: Who the hell are you?

1. The Schlumberger history is well recorded in Anne Gruner Schlumberger (1982), *The Schlumberger Adventure*, Arco Publishing. Gubkin Institute story: p. 70. Stalin's purges and nationalisation of assets: pp. 71–80.

Chapter 5: What makes a connection?

1. Jared Diamond (2012), *The World Until Yesterday: What can we learn from traditional societies?*, Viking Press. Ch. 1, 'Friends, Enemies, Strangers and Traders'.
2. For a short summary see 'John H. Patterson and the Sales Strategy of the National Cash Register Company, 1884 to 1922', Working Knowledge (1999), *Harvard Business Review*, https://hbswk.hbs.edu/item/john-h-patterson-and-the-sales-strategy-of-the-national-cash-register-company-1884-to-1922.
3. ibid.

Chapter 6: Instant rapport!

1. See *Story Meetings*, our online training course on story questioning and listening skills for first meetings, master.mysevenstories.com/courses/storymeetings.

2. Michael Bosworth and Ben Zoldan (2012), *What Great Salespeople Do*, p. 142.

3. *Story Prospecting* online course: using stories to find new clients, see master.mysevenstories.com/courses/storyprospecting.

4. See https://www.youtube.com/watch?v=EJjsjF1t3pc for a video record of the Bradford stadium fire. It's sobering viewing.

Chapter 7: Why you? Why your company?

1. Adapted from Adamson, Dixon, Spenner and Toman (2015), *Challenger Customer: Selling to the Hidden Influencer Who Can Multiply Your Sales Results*, Penguin.

2. The Political Bias Study 2006. Described in Wikipedia, https://en.wikipedia.org/wiki/Drew_Westen. Original article: Drew Westen, Pavel S. Blagov, Keith Harenski, Clint Kilts and Stephan Hamann (2006), 'Neural Bases of Motivated Reasoning: An fMRI Study of Emotional Constraints on Partisan Political Judgment in the 2004 U.S. Presidential Election', *Journal of Cognitive Neuroscience* (Massachusetts Institute of Technology) 18 (11).

3. Jonas T. Kaplan, Sarah I. Gimbel and Sam Harris (2016), 'Neural correlates of maintaining one's political beliefs in the face of counterevidence', *Scientific Reports* vol. 6, no. 39589.

4. Kaplan et al. (2017), 'Processing Narratives Concerning Protected Values: A Cross-Cultural Investigation of Neural Correlates', *Cerebral Cortex*, 27:1428–38.

5. Kevin Simler and Robin Hanson (2018), *The Elephant in the Brain*, Oxford University Press.

6. See the RAIN group corporate website at www.rainsalestraining.com/sales-training-programs.

7. See Schultz, Doerr and Rackham (2014), *Insight Selling: Surprising Research on What Sales Winners Do Differently*, Wiley.

8. The Corporate Executive Board (CEB) is now part of Gartner, www.cebglobal.com/about.html.

9. See https://en.wikipedia.org/wiki/Public%E2%80%93private_partnership for a description of the Public Private Partnership business model.

10. Paraphrased from Adamson, Dixon, Spenner and Toman (2015), *Challenger Customer*, p. 88.

11. Story sourced from https://en.wikipedia.org/wiki/Barry_Marshall and https://en.wikipedia.org/wiki/Robin_Warren.

Chapter 8: Be the only option

1. The Death of Alan Kurdi, https://en.wikipedia.org/wiki/Death_of_Alan_Kurdi. A stark and emotional image for anyone who sees it.

2. For a timeline on the European refugee situation and the impact of the media on public and political thinking, see www.infomigrants.net/en/post/4929/a-chronology-of-the-refugee-crisis-in-europe.

3. Albert Einstein (2014), *The World As I See It*, Snowball Publishing. A compilation of letters and articles from Einstein including from his teenage years' thought experiments. See also Walter Isaacson (2008), *Einstein: His Life and Universe*, Simon and Schuster.

4. Joseph Campbell (1949), *The Hero with a Thousand Faces*, Princeton: Princeton University Press.

5. Donald Miller (2017), *Building a Story Brand: Clarify your message so customers will listen*, HarperCollins.

6. Joseph Campbell calls this step 'meeting with the goddess' or supernatural aid. Your station in life as the guide is not so prosaic after all!

Chapter 9: The fight for your customer's mind

1. The *curse of knowledge* is a cognitive bias that occurs when an individual unknowingly assumes that others have the same background knowledge to understand them. https://en.wikipedia.org/wiki/Curse_of_knowledge.

2. Michael Bosworth and Ben Zoldan (2012), *What Great Salespeople Do*, pp. 142–3, from a Xerox study by Neil Rackham. Rackham claimed that you could 'set your watch by the 18 month slump in sales results'. They hypothesised that at that point the salesperson had learned the full range of products and their applications. The salesperson considered that they had seen all possible problems and so stopped listening and merely responded with a canned solution.

3. Alex Goldfayn (2015), *The Revenue Growth Habit: The simple art of growing your business by 15% in 15 minutes per day*, Wiley. In chapter 17, 'The art and science of getting the testimonial', Alex provides a detailed description of how to perform the 'client testimonial call'. This is also the perfect method for getting the client's stories. I highly recommend this book.

4. From Robert Cialdini, *The Psychology of Influence and Persuasion* (1984), p. 72, describing Freedman and Fraser's paper in the *Journal of Personality and Social Psychology*, 1966 (vol. 4, no. 2, 155–202).

Chapter 10: I submitted the proposal—now what?

1. Zig Ziglar (1984), *Zig Ziglar's Secrets of Closing the Sale*, Penguin Putnam, p. 32.

2. Neil Rackham (1988), *SPIN Selling*, McGraw-Hill.

3. Paraphrased from *SPIN Selling*, p. 25.

4. The term includes saleswomenship.

Chapter 11: Your buyer on remote control

1. The Corporate Executive Board, a sales advisory company, now part of Gartner. In 2017 the statistic was upgraded to almost seven decision makers. For a good overview of this subject, see https://hbr.org/2015/03/making-the-consensus-sale.

2. ABC News, 'Sydney Rail Service Restored to Normal', 1 May 2004, www.abc.net.au/news/2004-05-02/sydney-train-services-return-to-normal/179346.

3. For the origin of 'The HP Way', see www.hpalumni.org/hp_way.htm.

4. David Jacobson (1998), 'Founding Fathers', Stanford University Alumni review article, https://alumni.stanford.edu/get/page/magazine/article/?article_id=42103.

5. iPod and iTunes are trademarks of Apple Corporation.

6. I've been unable to find the origin of this saying.

Chapter 12: Influence in the dark

1. See this Wikipedia article for details on CarMax and their business mode: https://en.wikipedia.org/wiki/CarMax.

2. Richard Heller (2000), 'The Billionaire Next Door', *Forbes* magazine, www.forbes.com/global/2000/0807/0315036a.html#4d79bda44b69.

3. Private correspondence with Albert Goller, Siemens Australia CEO at the time.

4. Australia Industry Super Funds advertising campaign *You've Still Got Time*.

Index

Index

'True story. My twelve-year old daughter asked me what it takes to be successful in business. I reflected and responded that you must be alert to trends, street smart and be outstanding at sales. Selling yourself, your company and its key products. These things are not taught formally at schools.

'Storytelling is a fundamental part of selling. We all recall the sales guy that could break the ice with a joke but it's not the punch line, it's the way a story is narrated that really matters.

'I highly commend Mike Adams' book on storytelling. Even for my twelve year old!'

Michael Givoni. Portfolio Chairman, First5minutes, Winslow Construction and BSA Ltd.

'How did a former engineer sell over $1 billion worth of business during his sales career? This book is a must-read for salespeople.'

Matt Wanty. Author of *The Lost Art of Cold Calling*

'Mike's book is not only right place, right time with the right message, but it's undeniably accurate and supported by the science that Mike articulates so beautifully. Mike's Seven Stories Framework is both elegant and simple enough for every sales person to embrace. When they do, they will take their sales results to a whole new level. For sales people, the winners and losers of the future will be determined by their ability to use stories. This book is a must read for EVERY sales person in 2018 and beyond.'

Graham Hawkins. Founder and CEO SalesTribe

'Whatever line of business you're in, almost everyone nowadays is in the business of selling. It's also true that everyone hates being sold to... but everyone loves a story! Great stories transport us into other people's worlds, engaging emotion and bringing it to bear on a decision.

'The ability to tell a great story is arguably the most powerful tool in your toolbox. It differentiates the good from the great communicator and is at the very core of effective selling. Mike's book provides all you need to know to bring individual stores to life. Highly recommended.'

Malcolm Ferguson. Senior Sales Director, Oracle Australia

'As Mike says, "Stories are the secret weapon of the best salespeople." It is so true. Not only does he tell you what types of stories to tell, but he provides the "how"—with a framework and a story builder template. As a big fan of TED and The Moth, I've learned that telling stories is a craft, much like selling itself. When one can incorporate the fundamentals into sales opportunities that Mike guides you on, there is no doubt in my mind that more deals will come to closure and you and your company will be differentiated.'

Lori Richardson. President, Women Sales Pros, and CEO, Score More Sales

'Mike's book is a fantastic complement to the courses he runs on using the ancient art of storytelling to establish rapport and build confidence. Sales is a challenging profession, and in the modern electronic world, which seems to get faster every year, the art of promoting products or services through the use of a compelling and well-structured story is a powerful tool that for many has been forgotten. Mike is doing a fantastic job in reinvigorating this previously neglected skill. The framework of the seven types of stories is simple and easy to implement.'

Christopher Armstrong. Head of Markets and Growth, UGL

'In an era when we need to simplify the complex, storytelling is the conduit. This book brings insights and data together and shows us how to think differently and convey those thoughts effectively. It's about bringing back the long-lost art of true communication — stories! And it's a great primer for all business people, especially those who have a role to generate business.'

Bernadette McClelland. Author and CEO of 3 Red Folders

'Storytelling is rapidly becoming a lost art in sales, which is ironic since stories, metaphors and anecdotes are likely to be remembered long after the facts have been forgotten. Kudos to Mike Adams for shining a light on this very important selling skill.'

Tom Freese. President of QBS Research and author
of *The Secrets of Question-Based Selling*

'Mike Adams has years of experience in complex enterprise sales and distils his learnings into a framework that helps salespeople construct their company stories. It's a crucial skill that helps establish trust and build rapport. And it's the foundation for lasting business relationships. This book is a fantastic resource for sales and marketing professionals.'

Lee Bartlett. Author of *The No.1 Best Seller*

'I. Love. This. Book! Seven Stories Every Salesperson Must Tell *is a must-read for sellers and sales leaders. I'm continually preaching that our "sales story" is our most critical sales weapon, and Mike Adams does a masterful job expanding on not only WHY you need these seven types of stories, but HOW to create them. This book is so brilliantly put together that you will even get value from the Table of Contents. Read this and immediately put Adams' advice to work to increase your sales.'*

Mike Weinberg. Author of *New Sales. Simplified.*
and *Sales Management. Simplified.*

About Mike

Mike's *best* stories are not in this book. You'll need to ply him with wine and ask about the times in Siberia when his Russian host made a commercial airliner wait on the runway while drinking 'formalities' were completed. The stories *in* this book come from a surprisingly and perhaps unnecessarily challenging, multi-industry sales career whose only common threads have been good fortune and storytelling.

After living in nine countries, in 2002, when Chechen terrorists took 850 hostages in Moscow's Dubrovka Theatre siege, the police barricades went up outside Mike's office, where he had a perfectly good software sales manager role. Time to bring the family home.

Back in Australia, Mike told the best story of his career to land a job selling telecoms equipment. That led overseas again in 2007 to Malaysia, from where he managed more than a hundred sales and technical sales staff across Asia. The endless politics of a 60,000-staff corporate merger drove Mike back to the oil and gas industry—but he kept the same sales management territory (Asia), the same house and the same school for the boys, while his office, in the same building, moved up four levels to 75.

Schooling forced the next move back to Australia in 2012, this time with a job invitation to sell facility services into the mining townships and camps of remote Australia. Mike navigated two more industry changes after that—selling emergency communications equipment and then industrial products—before starting his consulting business.

With each industry change landing him on the wrong side of a steep learning curve with only a short time to succeed, Mike learned the value of seeking out and sharing specific persuasive stories. Now he finds stories and teaches storytelling to a client base as diverse and international as his own sales career.

Your Seven Stories

We offer a number of services to help you develop your own seven stories.

Seven Stories TV Channel

It's free to subscribe and you'll be kept up to date with our latest stories and story instruction: https://www.youtube.com/channel/UCRZrYSK_K6M8y0mxpqJLIUw.

Online Story Training

Courses provide video instruction, video stories, quizzes and exercises designed to help you become a master storyteller.

See master.mysevenstories.com/courses/sevenstories.

Story Sharing Facilitated Workshops

We offer full day and two-day workshops to teach your sales and marketing people storytelling. Ideal for sales kick-off meetings and conferences. Stories collected from these workshops form the basis for your new story library.

Story Consulting

Analyse your revenue strategy from a story perspective and create a story sales process, from prospect to satisfied customer. We help you research and refine your most important company stories and collect them in an online story library. Ask us about special-purpose programs for **new business development** and business expansion.

Bulk Book Orders for Your Sales Team

If you have enjoyed *Seven Stories* and found it useful, why not bulk order for your sales and marketing team? We **ship anywhere** in the world. Send us an email request.

Happy story sharing!

Mike Adams, June 2018
Mike.Adams@gifocus.com.au
Melbourne Australia
Connect on LinkedIn www.linkedin.com/in/m1keadams

Lightning Source UK Ltd.
Milton Keynes UK
UKHW010638151019
351641UK00002B/322/P